FORAGING

D1492825

First published 2009 by
Worple Press
PO Box 328
Tonbridge
Kent TN9 1WR

British Library Cataloguing in Publication data.
A catalogue record for this book is available from the British Library

ISBN 978 1 905208 12 8

Worple Press is an independent publisher specialising in poetry, art and
alternative titles. Worple Press can be contacted at:

Worple Press
PO Box 328
Tonbridge
Kent TN9 1WR

Tel: 01732 368958
E-mail: theworpleco@aol.com
Website: www.worplepress.co.uk

Typset and printed by Q3 Digital/Litho, Loughborough, Leicestershire

FORAGING

New and Selected Poems

James Aitchison

Other books by James Aitchison

Poetry
Sounds Before Sleep
Spheres
Second Nature
Brain Scans
Bird-Score

Criticism
The Golden Harvester: The Vision Of Edwin Muir

Reference
The Cassell Guide to Written English
The Cassell Dictionary of English Grammar

Edited, with Alexander Scott
New Writing Scotland Volumes 1, 2 and 3

CONTENTS

ACKNOWLEDGEMENTS

Since the publication of **Brain Scans** in 1998, new poems by James Aitchison have appeared in *Acumen*, *Agenda*, *Awen*, *Bard*, *Best Scottish Poems 2005* (Scottish Poetry Library web site), *Bird-Score*, *Black Mountain Review*, *A Book of Scottish Verse*, *Borderlines*, *Chanticleer Magazine*, *The Coffee House*, *The Coleridge Bulletin*, *Cumbria and Lake District Magazine*, *The Dark Horse*, *Decanto*, *The Edinburgh Book of Twentieth-Century Scottish Poetry*, *Essence Press website*, *The Herald*, *Kent & Sussex Poetry Anthology*, *Lines*, *The London Magazine*, *Moodswing*, *The New Criterion* (New York), *New Writing Scotland*, *Painted/spoken*, *The Poetry Library* (South Bank) *website*, *Poetry Monthly*, *Poetry Scotland*, *Quattrocento*, *The Reader*, *The Scottish Review*, *The SHOp*, *The Spectator*, *Third Anthology of Small Press Poets*.

FORAGING: NEW POEMS 1998 – 2008

For Norma, Blane, Karen, Nick and Cara

IN THE SOUTH

Votive in the past, both prayer and vow:
planting, mowing, hedging, barrowing.
His peasant rituals are irksome now
that vision and arteries are narrowing.

A task was like a penance in the north:
perform it voluntarily and you
in your small corner of the Carse of Forth
got absolution for a day or two.

The soil is heavier here in this Cotswold
garden, and weeds grow faster year by year.
But hand-weeding is still his surest hold
on the reality that lies out there.

His peasant at work says nothing, and that is why
his other, night self needs words' sanctity.
Words will be worth less if the peasant dies.

BLACKBIRD, HORSE, HARE

When we got out of the car on our first day
we saw in sudden close-up
a fallen blackbird with a twisted neck
and half-spread wings.
It must have died when it hit the window-pane.
All creatures lose their likeness when they die.

Most of our furniture was in store for months.

When we opened boxes of smaller things,
double bubble-wrapped in the other house,
the left hind leg of the wild-eyed leaping horse
and the right ear of the sitting hare
had broken off.

I didn't see you stick them on again,
the leg and the ear. Now I can hardly see
where the broken creatures have been repaired.

They're not like household gods, or family pets,
but horse and hare are lifelike once again.

Blackbirds are singing, singing for their lives
in the pear and chestnut trees of Hill Court Road.

FIVE DWARF FRUIT TREES

A small garden in Gloucestershire
lengthened in the camera's depth of field.
Gooseberry bushes
fantrained against a six-foot close-board fence
and clematis on a crumbly red-brick wall
seemed farther off than boot realities:
forking a lawn, uprooting cypress stumps.

And five dwarf fruit trees –
two old pears, a new Victoria plum,
new apple trees, a Worcester and a Cox –
looked almost orchard-like in the photographs.

The new trees made no growth.
The grafts were clean and the soil was fair
but temperatures reached thirty-five last summer,
hot enough to shrivel shallow roots.

You spoke of going north again:
rightmove, *primelocation*, *fish4homes*.

By the time we left,
the trees we'd planted were still too small to prune.

THE CHILD I WAS

In times of sickness and in times of pain
the child I was starts singing in my brain
some hymns he sang aged ten at school. He sings
of all things bright and beautiful ... all things ...
a green hill far away ... of snow on snow
in bleak midwinters now and long ago.
He sings these hymns as pagan healing songs
to make me well again. I sing along.

In times of failure and in times of fear
the child I was reaches across the years
and takes my hand in his, a child aged ten.
I have less courage now than he had then.
How can I put all childish things away?
The child who sings and holds my hand will stay.
We understand each other now. The child
I was, the child I am, are reconciled.

WALLS HAVE EARS

'Walls Have Ears,' the wartime poster warned.
Indoors, our walls were bare but were adorned
with love and care and the ordinary cries
of children. No. This isn't an exercise
in nostalgia: my two-room childhood home
was bulldozed fifty years ago, a slum.

Two rooms, a fireplace, one cold-water tap.
And German spies immured there to entrap
us? Or were they walled in our backyard
communal lavatory? We had to guard
our words and sometimes had to keep our mouths
shut because the plain war-time home truths —
ours was a common home and family —
could have comforted an enemy.

FORAGING

You checked your gas mask in its cardboard box,
counted the coupons in our ration books
and then went tracking rumour from shop to shop.
McAndrew's? Just a row of meatless hooks
and sawdust without bloodstains. No fresh fruit
in Campbell's: 'The hail aipple/pear/plum crop
went to the Forces. Turnip, hen? Beetroot?'

Some days you reached the end of your pursuit.
In overall coats that hadn't been cut from jute
sacks but had a starch-fresh pre-war look,
women sliced cheese with wire in the Co-op,
pat-patted butter into half-pound blocks
and stacked small bars of pink carbolic soap.
Foraging is a force older than hope.

DEATH …

You vomited blood again, and were discharged
unfit for service in the Engineers
or any regiment. When you emerged
from hospital on your diet of steamed fish,
porridge and milk, you might have thought you'd years
and years ahead of you. And then your wish
for us – a new house, garden, and a lease
that's ours – came true! Beyond the boundary
fence, a burn's clear waterflow, a peace
of open fields, skylarks and a wide sky
on the horizon. But the strong new growth
you felt was cancer spreading through your brain
like god in his old role as psychopath.
At Easter-time you were released from pain.

… AND TRANSFIGURATION

I was too terrified to join the men
who lowered your coffin into earth that day
in 1948 when I was ten
years old, and I'm still trying to repay
the debt. Perhaps my years of fearfulness
were just a version of the normal ills
of growing up, but I felt fatherless,
unfathered by your early death, until … ?

There was no sudden change, no leap of faith.
Time transformed you to your transmundane
yet natural condition of life-in-death:
arrays of living networks in my brain.

You sit up, smile, alive on your deathbed
like a forgiving god inside my head.

PATHÉ NEWS

Strange people stood behind a prison fence
gazing at him, reaching with one hand
and with the other hand holding a strand
of wire as if they had to hold on or fall.

They were wearing torn pyjamas and ragged shawls.
The Pathé Pictorial newsreel made no sense:
pyjamas in daytime, in the open air?
Where were all their day clothes? Didn't they care?

The Western was next; he had to stay.
These funny people …? He knew he couldn't be seen
by them because their eyes were far away,
but he felt looked at as he watched the screen.

The newsreel showed a pile of knobbly logs.
Logs … ? No, not logs, but heaped-up people so thin
and bare they looked like logs. And through their skin
the boy could see the framework of their bones.

Skin … bones… Just skin and bones. Just skeletons.
The odd bits sticking out were arms and legs.
And then a great big pile of empty shoes …
He couldn't understand the Pathé news.

THE LAWS OF CHILDHOOD

The laws of childhood are the magic laws:
transmutants, witches, fairies, Santa Claus,
spells for making time go slow or fast.
By law a dreaming child re-incarnates
the brain's immortal, polymorphous beast.
Cosmic monsters are his intimates.

A sleeping child who feels the night beast's breath
begins to know how close life is to death:
the beast might eat him up before his screams
are heard. The waking child still bears the weight
of law; the child in daylight as in dreams
already knows how close love is to hate.

> A child has a twin self, a secret other
> closer than brother, sister, father, mother.
> He loves the loving secret self above
> all else, and yet he re-enacts the sin:
> a child must find himself, a child must prove
> himself by killing off the secret twin.

> A single self is not enough to bear
> the laws' full weight, is not enough to share
> the pain. But having killed the other self,
> he fears the voices talking in his head,
> multiple selves that call across the gulf,
> the dead twin rising tenfold from the dead.

The laws of childhood are the laws of nature;
a child is both a human and brute creature.
A child's brain is measurably small;
a child's mind is immeasurably vast
beyond the powers of other animals –
fabulous futures, confabulated pasts.

The laws of childhood cannot be repealed;
the laws are indissolubly annealed
in those first memories that shape the mind.
We have survived, but none of us outgrows
the child he was, for no one can rescind
the magical and natural childhood laws.

THE LOST KINGDOM

Phantasmagoric beasts appear
in children's dreams to teach them fear.
Across the widening abyss
of memory I remember this.

A monkey in my picture book
woke up one night and came to look
at me as I slept in my bed.
A monkey screamed inside my head.

I must have been aged three or four.
I remember nothing before
the picture of that chimpanzee
drove me from my infancy.

How could we dance before we walked?
How could we sing before we talked?
How could I talk before I knew
that I was I and you were you?

Brown chimpanzee? Orang utan?
Till my self-consciousness began
we shared the same intelligence.
I don't remember innocence.

A BOY

He swelters in a tedium of stopped time,
an endless interim of here and now.

'Cross-cross, criss-cross, criss-cross three times and spit.'
The laws of magic are less magical.

Each year on his birthday and Christmas Day
more criss-cross places in his mind close down.

A self breaks with the breaking of his voice.
At home he's billeted with aliens.

He can hear snowflakes falling.
He can't be moved to tears by melodies.

The boy knows sadness but when Grandpa died
he giggled at the oddity of death.

MISS CARLSON SAID

'The swirling? That's the life force in Van Gogh's trees,'
Miss Carlson said. 'And the shuddering in his soul.'

He walks home in the rain and doesn't get wet.

'Memory and dreams,' Miss Carlson said,
'are truer than any camera.'

A bit of his brain is playing bass guitar.

'In Venice I paint the fish market,' she said.
'Fish like lungs and guts pulse on the slab.'

There's paint beneath Miss Carlson's fingernails
and in the fine-grain wrinkles of her finger skin.

The bass is thudding in echo chambers of his brain.

'*Mont Sainte-Victoire* – each version is a universe,'
Miss Carlson said. 'And you can enter it.'

Miss Carlson's fingernails are plain, square-cut.
Her wrists are very thin.

Next time it snows he'll try to piss her name.

GIRLS CALLED IMOGEN

A paler band of skin across his wrist …?
He must have left it in the changing-room
while he was dreaming that he'd kissed
Imogen Smith's nipples and teased a comb
through her curled hair. His wrist-watch …? Old Bert checks
for mobiles, coins, keys, litter, chewing-gum
between one PE lesson and the next.

Self falls apart from self; his loose selves swirl
like snowflakes in a shaken paperweight.
He hasn't spoken to the girl.
The watch he left behind is accurate.
He isn't who he was a week ago.
'For God's sake, Daniel! Hurry up! You're late.'
Brain time, mind time is always fast or slow.

Daniel can't help acting like a fool
when Imogen's around: the butterflies
and frogs, the cataracts, the whirlpools.
He knows his foolish mask's a thin disguise
for love's insanity. He doesn't know old men
as well as boys – The colour of her eyes …?
still fall in love with girls called Imogen.

SLIDING

When I was small there was a winter rule:
if films of ice or furry layers of frost
covered the playground of my primary school
we had to make a slide. Line up, run fast,
half-turn, knees braced and feet apart to ride
the impetus of ice until the slide
breached playground walls and reached across sixty years.

Side-on, knees braced and feet apart I skim
the smooth, wide treads of a final flight of stairs,
glissading down through a recurring dream
so plainly physical it feels like fact.

When sliding childhood memories coincide
with adult dreams, a little code is cracked.
A poem leaves the mystery intact.

WAITING-ROOM

Two-fifty. My appointment is for three.
I try to shut it out but fear admits
itself and fills my mind; not fear in me
but me inside the fear. I can't outwit
this surfeit of electrochemistry.
Is fear a form of moral deficit?

The lump's benign. The surgeon's little blade
should cut as easily as I disbud
a rose. And yet…? Reason turns renegade.
Imagination could spark the photo-flood
that once eclipsed my mind. I am afraid
there's no escape from fear; it's in the blood.

Fear gorges on the kind of time that waits
in waiting-rooms. I know what brings my dread:
a neurotransmitter breaches the sluice gates
of synapses and sense inside my head
where time slows down as fear accelerates.
It's too late now to ask for a pre-med.

Small knowledge of my mind is no defence
against this variation on the same
old theme. I can't walk out because my sense
of fear would be compounded with the shame —
it's more than just a secular offence —
of being absent when they call my name.

SPEECHLESS

I lose my notes and don't know what to say.
They're faceless in my dreams, the students I face.

In fact, I always had explicit scripts
and handouts for key words and names and dates.
I couldn't lecture without a jacket and tie;
I never sat down; I stood as still as I could:
evangelical, confrontational.

I'm summoned by the academic board;
I cancel lectures for that afternoon.
'Ah, Dr Aitchison. Give us your account.
Don't mention language, mind or poetry.'

I dream and live the same anxieties,
part vanity, part craving and part fear.

I don't like dreaming, living in the past
but it's all around me now.
Awake, asleep, I don't dream hard enough.

One way of counting time is the tense of verbs,
especially the future in the past:
'He was a promising young poet once
but a few years later he was to become … '

My dreams are how I lived ten years ago.
The board ruled that my language and my mind
were out of order. Perhaps the board was right:
ten years, and I'm still dreaming speechless dreams.

When I wake up I shall forget all this.

DEAF

He hears you talking but he doesn't hear
all the words your speech sounds represent.
He listens hard: the wordless words pass by.
He can't locate their whatsits …? Referents?
The nameless things your lost words signify.

He can decode the spoken word below
a given frequency, but women's speech –
soft-voiced sopranos – and the odd phonemes
of regional accents are beyond his reach.
He's listening, but he can't make out your names.

The faults lie in the workings of his ears:
they don't. He'd know exactly what you meant
if he could still infer what you imply.
But deaf old men grow unintelligent:
you ask straight questions; they give bent replies.

Some conversations are more ebb than flow
for him: meanings adrift, voices off-pitch.
You think the deaf old man's mind is as dim
as his hearing. Hard to know which is which.
He answers questions no one puts to him.

WAKING, SLEEPING, DREAMING

'I cannot certainly distinguish waking
from sleeping,' Descartes wrote. 'In sleep I feel
and think of non-existent things that seal
themselves into a mind forever making
reality so dream-like, dreams so real.'

The self who dreams and in the act of dreaming
knows that he dreams and knows he will reclaim
the dream when he awakes, can't be the same
self as the one who dreams and wakes up screaming
because he doesn't know that it's a dream.

When you're asleep you can't know that you're sleeping
and yet part of your brain is still at work
and still, perhaps, awake. A tiny spark
of light in your nonconsciousness is keeping
your sleeping self alive all through the dark.

I dream that someone in my dream's pretending
he's me. A trick of light? A hologram?
But since the dream is mine, I'm both the sham
and the real me. I wake up apprehending
less than I dreamt of who I really am.

He couldn't get to sleep some nights for hating.
Himself, mainly. He used to get up, drink,
and smoke and write until he couldn't think
straight or even crookedly. Now sleep's waiting
to lead him quietly across the brink.

TASKS AND CALIBAN

Each time my sleeping Caliban
awakes he fouls my mind and basks
in my polluted memory.

I live as quietly as I can.
I know containment is a task
as hard as any poetry.

TOO FAR

I live as quietly as I can. I fear
hysteria, but once or twice a year
I go too far, the only way I know
of finding how far I can safely go.

Not far. Not far. And not for long, because
too far might have no limits and no laws.
I'm too soft now to think of living rough
and yet I know too far's not far enough.

Timidity creates this minor art;
too far is where true poetry should start.

ELECTION

Election night: we waited for the count.
My Scottish Liberalism was treachery
for one supporter of the S.N.P.:
'You English bastard, you! You English cunt!'

It wasn't party politics, of course.
What my opponent feared was the way I spoke.
I should have known my accent could provoke
his hatred. There was reason in his curse.

Fifty years ago I made a choice:
I mimicked actors reading poetry
on the Third Programme of the BBC
and then I hid my self inside a voice.

I rejected my native dialect:
intonation contours' pitches, rhythms,
idiomatic glottal Scotticisms
until I'd reconditioned my vocal tract.

I wanted to disguise myself, not flaunt
those playback vowels: monophthong, diphthong.
The S.N.P. man heard a foreign tongue
that night. And there was justice in his taunt.

THE SEA SO CALM, THE SEA SO ROUGH

ABERDEEN TO STROMNESS

Sky and sea grew more serene
as we sailed farther north,
cerulean, aquamarine,
across the Pentland Firth.

A moving ship creates a chill
wind, but the air was warm.
The sea so calm, the sea so still
I saw just one waveform.

I watched it from the afterdeck,
a luminescent stream
of liquid marble, the ship's wake,
viridian and cream.

I sailed across a boundary,
imagination's rim;
too sudden a delight for me
to join the seraphim.

And as we passed through Scapa Flow
late in the afternoon,
I saw an archipelago
of stars and crescent moon.

Sun and moon shone till the night
at last nudged out the day.
The islands' twinkling warning lights
were like a galaxy

I'd sailed beyond the farthest edge
of my experience
into a saintless pilgrimage
of joy and penitence.

A way of seeing can recall
from dream and memory
the world that was before the fall,
the first reality.

STROMNESS TO ABERDEEN, OVERNIGHT

An inner cabin, not twin berths
but bunks. I thought the one on top
too risky for the Pentland Firth;
I was afraid that I would drop
out when I dropped off. I placed
the top bunk's bedding on the floor
and lay down in the narrow space,
my feet against the cabin door.

The stabilizers were withdrawn
less than an hour out of Stromness,
the sea so rough it would have torn
the stabilizers off. Wingless,
St Sunniva was plunging, yawing
in wind force seven on Beaufort's scale,
rolling, wallowing and sea-sawing.
Beaufort's force seven's a moderate gale.

When I switched off the cabin light
in seas so rough, in dark so dense,
at once I lost my power of sight
but found again my childish sense
of being: how to be so small
and still I couldn't suffer harm.
Tomorrow I would reach landfall
despite the violence of the storm.

It wasn't just the dark that shrank
my mind: the only way to sleep,
half-sleep, that night was two-thirds drunk.

I used the other third to keep
time with the engines' regular
beat. But arrhythmic seas would heave
like flotsam the *St Sunniva*
above the level of the waves.

Its stern clear of the waterline,
its engines and my heart would skip
two or three beats. The screws would whine
on air until the rearing ship
fell down again, and down, and down
from a high crest into a trough.

And yet I knew we wouldn't drown.
My shrunken mind was drunk enough
to sail me safely through the rough
night seas into a sober dawn.

DIPPER TERRITORY

For Gerry Cambridge

A subliminal pre-sighting? Before I can say
'This could be dipper territory,'
I see the whirring ball of russet, white
and grey go flicker-skimming across the stream.
It settles on a boulder, folds it wings,
and nods itself, twitches and bobs itself
into the bibbed roundness of a dipper.

When it walks under water
the dipper defies its natural buoyancy,
defies the force of the downrush, the weight of cold.
It walks beneath the watersongs
of plunge and gulp, laughter-splash, guttural chattering
and a crystalline song like chiming icicles.
When the bird rises again, its feathers are dry.

Dippers live by rivers' origins.
Their presence proves the cleanliness of air
and earth and water in these fissured uplands.
They seldom venture downstream.
I could live without dippers. They can live
only if I keep some part of my mind
clean enough to be their habitat.

BLACKBIRD SONGS

Sometimes at dusk a blackbird calls in fright –
not the pulsating, ululant daytime shriek
but the frequentative think-think, think-think,
before it settles down – think-think – to roost,
as if it knew the terrors that the night
might bring: cat, tawny owl, or feral mink,
a wind from the north-east, a late hard frost.

Guidebooks say it has a fluting tone,
the song the blackbird sings by day; but words
can't re-create its music. The song's unique,
and yet I hear it in the other Bird's
slow passages, when Parker's saxophone
cries like an inevitable force
of nature. Listen. Hear the human mind
and a bird's brain making the same kind
of music from the same mysterious source.

Music is imperative, innate
in the two species; but it would be wrong
to say that the two musics are the same
or even variations on a theme.
To make our music we have to translate
the urging across layer upon layer
of self and consciousness that separate
us from the prehistoric internet
of the unthinking universal dream.

The blackbird's is the truly natural song.
The bird is music, instrument, and player.

MUTE SWANS

Not mute, of course. Swans hiss their outstretched hate
at anything that might be predator.
And I've heard swan's-breath sigh, a crooning purr.

Feel their flagellant, frenzied piston-gait
when they tread water, walk on water, run
on water to heave their flapping bulk from one
element into another.
                      Swans in flight
stroke the mute air so that in time it sings
the perfect feathersong of beating wings.

Their awkward, waddling, ill-proportioned weight
on land dissolves in water. Swans displace
their dry grotesquerie with liquid grace.

In stillness they reflect immaculate
concepts: their coupled ease of complex arcs,
seraphic answers to their question marks.

CROW AND ASH TREE IN APRIL

When other trees are green this tree's still grey.
Its buds don't burst until the end of May.
Each year a few more branches die away.

The crow soared to the crown and clamped its beak
on the base of a black-tipped twig but it couldn't break
or cut the twig away.
                              The crow's mistake
was to confuse the living and the dead:
the leaflessness, perhaps, or blackness led
the crow to act is if the twig's black bead
were lifeless.
                              When it knew it couldn't rip
the twig out, the crow flapped, cawed, changed its grip
and clamped its beak tight on the ash twig's tip.

The crow bounced up and down. It was the same
crow but now it had a different aim:
not nest-sticks but this springing spring-time game.

The crow was playing in its bird-brained way,
instinctive and involuntary play:
crow brain cells stirred; the bird had to obey.

I have free will, and yet I do not know
why I have the feeling that I owe
a poem to an ash tree and a crow.

WRENS

After mild winters wrens can be as numerous as sparrows,
and yet even in good years they seem rare:
they never flock and seldom appear as a pair.

They share the same gardens as robins
but not robins' daring.
Wrens can't shake off the tic of fear.

I watch one quivering on the stone gatepost,
not cold but shivering, nerves twitching,
a frightened traveller between flights,
neither perching nor hovering on the gatepost.

It darts unwaveringly into the cover of the beech hedge.
Seconds later the hedge bursts into song.

WAXWINGS

Waxwings have brain enough
to know they'll starve and freeze if the north-east wind
blows for a day, a day and another day.
In simple mindless matters of life or death
instinct is the only way of knowing.

But how do they know there will be berries here
on hawthorn, holly and pyracantha trees,
contoneaster, rowan or dog rose?
And how do they know the way? How do they know
the angle of the sun on sunless days?

They're driven by hunger, not farsightedness,
windblown from Norway over the North Sea
to Lothian, Lincolnshire, East Anglia.

Or is one bird-brain part of a flock-size brain,
and the flock obeys a blind intelligence?
If finding berries were simply a matter of chance
how long would waxwings live?

Blackbirds here pick fruit from the crown of a tree
bead by bead over weeks or even months
down to the lower branches.
Waxwings strip a tree in one perched hour.

PARADISE LOST

His eyes itch; they weep rainbows edged with fire.
His pupils are blind with light as if he'd turned
a telescope towards the midday sun.

Dead retinas, or severed optic nerves?
Irises and aqueous humour are burned
opaque. And yet beneath the occipital bone
the cortex of his vision is entire.

This is no common blindness but blindsight.
His mind creates what mind alone observes:
a universe above the golden filth
of kings, beyond the orbit of desire.

The blind man spoke, scribes wrote, God countersigned
new laws for a celestial commonwealth,
the cosmic statutes of John Milton's mind.

*　*　*　*　*

Paradise Lost and the First World War: Compare.
Imperial armies, millions of volunteers,
more millions waiting for the call from Haig.
Fifty thousand lives for half a mile
of some blood-cratered sodden foreign field.
Night flares like falling stars in No-Man's-Land.
Victoria would have wept, and called for more.

Milton is faster, vaster, better lit.
Infinite angels rush from Heaven to Hell.
Some stay. Others fly back at God-think speed:
in *Paradise Lost* that's twice the speed of light.

Haig, like Milton, had his cherubim:
troupes of smartly uniformed telegraph boys –
'No whistling!' – pedalling news from street to street.

* * * * *

I should be reading *Paradise Lost*, Book Four.
Instead, I'm stacking supermarket shelves
and deep-freeze cabinets to pay the fees.
The re-stock plan is like an A-to-Z
street map. I'm doing fruit and veg tonight:
organic artichokes, banana hands,
two hundred heads of Albanian broccoli,
ten kilos of zucchini from God-knows-where.

Robots will be doing this job next year.
No, not androids; intelligent fork-lift trucks.
It isn't just the money; it's the perks:
fast-food freebies past their sell-by dates.

Book Four? Five? Six? Who gives a shit these days?
Megafuckingstructural cosmic maze!

THE HOWLING WILDERNESS: COLERIDGE'S DREAMS

'While I am awake, by patience, employment, effort of mind, &
walking I can keep the fiend at Arm's length; but the Night is my Hell,
Sleep my tormenting Angel. Three Nights out of four I fall asleep,
struggling to lie awake – & my frequent Night-screams have almost
made me a nuisance in my own House. Dreams with me are no
Shadows, but the very Substance & foot-thick Calamities of my Life.'
Coleridge to Thomas Wedgwood, September 1803

'Pray for me, my dear Allsop! that I may not pass such another night as
the last. While I am awake & retain my reasoning powers, the pang is
gnawing but I am – except for a fitful moment or two – tranquil – It is
the howling Wilderness of Sleep that I dread.' Coleridge to Thomas
Allsop, July 1820.

What fiend? What angel? Coleridge doesn't say.
As evil as snake-goddess Geraldine?
Even by the reasoning light of day
he was afraid to name what he had seen.

    A poet's imagination mediates
    between two states of being: chaos and grace,
    like Christ who comes between a God who hates
    and God whom you can trust when you confess.

Because he knew some of the many ways
in which his mind worked, Coleridge tried to keep
himself awake all night. He knew the day's
anxieties would grow monstrous in his sleep.

By day or candle-light his waking thought
confined the monster to its far domain.
But when he slept, its natural habitat
was in the howling places of his brain.

A poet's imagination can naturalize
the supernatural creatures of nightmare.
But if the poet's imagination dies
then he has small defence against despair.

The more he prayed that he would stay awake,
the more dream-terrors grew until his God
was less majestic than the naked snake-
goddess who throbbed through Coleridge's life-blood.

Time passed. He lived his mind's life more in prose
than poetry. Had years of opium
poisoned the well? Or was a poem too close
to madness and his dreams' delirium?

If poems and dreams emerge from the same source –
mind's borderland, land of the pythoness –
then to make a poem was to curse
himself into that howling wilderness.

Some poets find the meanings of their dreams
in truths that their imaginations prove
in the waking trance. Those poets' themes
are craft, art, chance, humility, and love.

A poet's imagination – Is it faith
or is it a state of mind beyond belief?
In Coleridge it's a dare-all dance with death.
The howling wilderness was half his life.

ALMOST A REMEMBRANCE

'I think Poetry should strike […] the Reader as a wording of his own
highest thoughts, and appear almost a Remembrance.' To John Taylor,
February 1818

Our raw encounters, incidents, accidents
become experience
through reason, imagination and memory,
the only way
for readers as for poets. But poets dare
more devils. Readers share
in the itinerary on the page
but it's the poet who makes the pilgrimage
across a chasm he himself creates
before he can unlock the gates.
A poem's uncertain wordless genesis
is in the mind's abyss.

The poet steps off in the faith
that chance and etymology and myth
will map the territory beyond
imagination's present borderland.
And what a poem charts,
a journey's end, is where the reader starts.

He reads. He hears the text
inside his head and thinks he recollects
the experience. He reads the poet's mind
and thinks his thoughts. He finds
false memories of things he knows are true,
remembrances of worlds he never knew.

BY SENSATION AND WATCHFULNESS

'The Genius of Poetry must work its own salvation in a man: It cannot
be matured by law and precept, but by sensation & watchfulness in
itself.' To John Augustus Hessey, October 1818

A poem begins as consciousness began:
without a grammar or a lexicon.

When we felt some sensations re-appear –
flight, hunger, falling, rage, the smell of fear –
long after the event, just as the dead
come and go inside a living head,
then we found consciousness and time. Or they
found us, made us their watchers and their prey.
The dead outlive themselves, sensations outlast
themselves and make a future of the past.

We grew more watchful. We became aware
of watching night-eyes watch us: wolf, lynx, bear.
And watching over us, for we could feel
spirits of stars and waterfalls as real
as running water. But we couldn't bless
our new sensations, our new watchfulness
in the old ways: through fire, blood, chant and dance.

We needed some new kind of utterance
to meet the mysteries; not grunt, howl, shriek,
growl, cackle, hiss. Then we began to speak.

WIND

'Notwithstanding your Happiness and your recommendation I hope I
shall never marry. […] The roaring of the wind is my wife, and the
Stars through the window pane are my Children.' To George and
Georgiana Keats, October 1818

He's married to an autumn wind that roars
through clashing branches of the sycamores
and scatters their last leaves across the sky.
And like the wind among the sycamore boughs,
a roaring wife can strain a husband's vows
to breaking point. But every wind will die
away. When he's delivered from the storm
the poet is at liberty to form
new unions that seem brief and yet defy
the centuries; for when a poet binds
himself in words he also binds our minds
to his. And he is freely bound to try
wife after wife: a man who has been kissed
by poetry is a constant bigamist.

STARS

Except in that near-equinoctial light
of an autumn evening or late afternoon
when we might see the zodiacal arc
of stars and planets, sun and crescent moon,
we cannot see the stars until the night
is all around us and the skies are dark.

Children, Keats called them, because their domain
was also his: he stared at the night skies
and found a way of looking through the pane
as if the universe flowed from his eyes.
We come from stardust; stardust's in our veins
and in the microcosm of our brains.

And when a star burns out it shines for years,
light-years, before its starlight disappears.

WITHOUT THIS FEVER

'I want to compose without this fever. I hope one day I shall.' To
George and Georgiana Keats, September 1819

Fever was fervour. It was no disease
of mind but that condition – sure, perplexed –
of falling unconditionally in love
day after day with poems he had to write.
He was be-mused, and nothing can appease
a poet's need, not this poem or the next
or next again. He knew he had to prove
his love by ordeal, imagination's white
hot fire. But could he by time's slow degrees
have cooled his fever and kept his intellect's
pure flame intact? Whatever power drove
his fevered mind to visionary sight –
a power the other fever couldn't seize –
is still in force. We read him by its light.

'We are for ever talking of the peace and order which prevail under a Government which is for ever at war somewhere or other.' William Howard Russell (Russell of *The Times*) 1820-1907

Navvies, they call themselves, because they toil
like navigators excavating soil
to make a great canal. They dig so deep
they cannot throw the soil over the steep
banks, and so they make an earthen ramp.
Up and down all morning the navvies tramp.
'Big enough to float the Royal barge,'
said the sergeant navigator in charge.

*   *   *   *   *

Two armies closed till English seemed the same
as Russian. I saw no stratagem
other than blood. The men fought hand-to-hand
till nightfall. Now they lie in no-man's-land
more than a mile away and yet the sounds
of screaming reach me from the killing ground.
I cannot tell the screams of Russians
from English, or a horse's from a man's.

The rescue squad will set out at first light.
We can do nothing for the men tonight
except make ready rescuers and tools:
the sailcloth sacks, the wooden sleds, the mules,
the harness, coils of rope, a length of chain,
water, rifles, bayonets. And then
at dawn with bayonets fixed the rescue squad
will march towards the wounded and the dead.

Deep wounds fester like slow fires that burn
all night until the bright red bloodstains turn

black. Black blood congeals in ruptured lungs.
The gaping mouths are filled with blackened tongues.
Scutari? Typhoid, cholera, the plague
of gangrenous maggots? The men's eyes beg
for the one cure they know will slake their thirst:
the sudden mercy of the bayonet thrust.

With ordinary care they would have lived,
those men, those hundreds of men who survived
the battle yesterday but had to lie
between the lines all night because a thigh
was broken, or a shin-bone, or a foot.
Water, a bandage, blanket or greatcoat –
they would have lived with ordinary care.
Instead, they bled and burned beneath the stars.

*   *   *   *   *

A navvy bends his back to take the weight;
he leans into a rapid shuffling gait
that takes him down the ramp, and there he shrugs
the canvas sack to earth. A navvy drags
the sack the last few inches into square
rank after rank and layer upon dead layer
until the great canal is filled with sails.
It is the navigator who prevails.

LINES FOR FRED ASTAIRE

For Gordon and Mary Lang

A bean-pole body, big ears, thinning hair.
'You haven't got the form or face that fits
the screen,' producers said to Fred Astaire
(originally Frederick Austerlitz.)
'You were a star back east in *Lady Be Good*
and *Funny Face*. But this is Hollywood,
Fred. Hollywood. Forget your Broadway hits.'

And that is why he practised elegance
each day until the energy and grace
he sought became innate, and he could dance
above the dragging gravities of place
and time to any rhythm, any pace.

Rewind. Replay. It doesn't matter where
you stop the tape: he dances in mid-air.

SEER, SHAMAN

Stallion's nerve ends ripple-twitch across its flanks
where horseflies stab and suck.
Veins bulge along its head.
Huge eyes swivel, oozing translucencies.

Buzzard's garnet eyes
reflect, absorb, magnify
all scurryings
and the hush of carrion.

Starlings in flight are kinetic geometries
of shrilling madcap curves and arcs and gyres.
They fly to the remote control
of a prehistoric choreographer,
lord of dancing flocks, swarms, shoals and clouds.
Down to earth,
a thousand black-green violets iridesce
on each bird's wing.

His crow is the only crow in the world
and all the crows the world has ever known.

Seer, shaman,
his mind is habitat for natural things.
Wolf, nightjar, grasshopper and daffodil
are made from the same stardust, sun and clay
as humans and gods.

'Churchill? I saw his funeral on t.v.
and so it can't be him. Who bombed Suez?
Who wanted Farouk – Tommy Copper fez
and all – back on the throne? Eden? Attlee?
Attlee smoked a pipe and drank strong tea.'

Regions of her mind that should be here
and now are uninhabitable. Her brain
is shrinking. Memories won't come back again.
She has lived safely in the past for years,
but now her past begins to disappear.

'Mac-something. Very old. Somebody Mac …
You? No. No. You're the man who cannot name
the prime minister. But you mustn't blame
yourself. We all forget, we all lose track
of names from time to time, but they'll come back.'

Indignity? Her visible decay?
Your mother will know nothing. You'll feel worse
than she. She's on a journey in reverse:
to babbling childhood, speechless infancy
and then, as I believe, eternity.

'I know that I forget, but when you know,
you know it's only absentmindedness.
That winter. Weeks and months of Christmases.
And those men who smoked pipes? Where did they go?
I was still young enough to love the snow.'

FRANCES SOMERS' DREAMS

IN THE GARDEN

I cup my hand, I grip, I turn my wrist
and pluck ripe apples from brittle-knuckled twigs.
A real garden and trees. The fruit's the dream:
big, round, shapely apples, their crimson skin
anointed with an aromatic sheen.

I wrap them in paper tissues one by one.
I go to layer them in a cardboard box:
the tissues open, the apples unripen, shrink
to bitter green. A thinning, not a crop.

The dream tells me to put them back on the trees.
The dream and I know it's impossible.
I try: the apples fall out of the dream.

IN THE CINEMA

I'm an usherette in a mini-cinema.
Usherette? Are they still called usherettes?
I'm sitting on my little tip-up seat.
The projection room is just above my head.

The dream is telling me to watch the film
and telling me I've seen the film before.
I've seen them all before;
I know what happens next in all of them.

Last showing of the night. The end.
The audience leaves before the lights come up.
The empty cinema is smaller now.

Lights are dimmed again. The projectionist upstairs –
we've never met but we understand each other –
projects the rewind onto the screen.

Rewind. Fast backwards. Stop. Fast backwards. Stop.
There's no soundtrack. Everyone's doing it,
a stop-start silent Charlie Chaplin walk.

They're going back to the beginning, everyone,
for the first house tomorrow afternoon.

IN THE RESTAURANT

A birthday lunch in the rooftop restaurant.
My sixtieth-birthday lunch; I'm sixty-three.
My birthday's in June;
it's late November in the dream.
The restaurant is real:
the top floor of the Carlton George Hotel.

SORRY. LIFTS OUT OF ORDER. PLEASE USE STAIRS.

I enter the stairwell and begin to climb
in timeless dream-time. I reach the restaurant.
White islands floating in a blue lagoon;
only one of them is set, and set for one.

'The others have cancelled, madam, but you will stay.'
He hands me the menu.
'Lunch is on the house. Enjoy the view.'

Domes, spires, rooftops, smokeless chimney pots.
Seeing from above is looking down.
I look up: no signs, no absurdities.
Coal fires and starlings were banished years ago.

The dream is too intelligible for dreams.

I don't remember eating anything.

HIDE AND SEEK

We play at hide and seek. I'm always the one.
No. This isn't another dream. It's fact.
Or was. I'll use the present tense as if …
When I play at hide and seek with my grandchildren
I'm the one. That way there's less quarrelling.

'Ninety-nine, one hundred. Here I come!'

They hide in the same few places every time
and I pretend that Piers and Imogen –
Piers is four and Imogen is seven –
have disappeared. They'd rather hide than seek.
They like to run away, but not too far.

Imogen was my angel till Piers was born.
She hated him: 'I want Piers to get dead.'

And so I have to guess how long to search
wrong places in the garden.
Sometimes I walk around unseen
till Piers and Imogen fear they're lost,
so far away they'll never be found again.

I hear them arguing behind the lavender hedge.
I cry, 'I spy Piers and Imogen.'

MOONBEAM RADIO

For seventeen years I lived by selling time:
'Take to the air and watch your profits climb.'
In Tele-sales my mission was to entice
new clientèle by selling time half-price,
and give the kiss of life to dead accounts
by promising lapsed clients top discounts –
forty per cent off Maxine's Morning Show –
when they returned to Moonbeam Radio.

When, not if. If wasn't in my book.
No ifs or buts. And that was how I broke
all records for new revenues from cold
calls, and lost sheep brought back to the fold
of Moonbeam Radio. I was at my peak.
And then … I don't … And then I had to speak
faster, faster, for time was running slow.
Not me, but time, and Moonbeam Radio.

You don't say *nervous breakdown* nowadays.
It's *affective disorder*; that's the phrase
you use. But something breaks. Perhaps your heart.
Your spirit and your will are torn apart.
Torn? Broken? Anyway, they disappear.
That afternoon when I burst into tears
and couldn't stop, they called in Doctor Lowe,
the doc retained by Moonbeam Radio.

'Time. Rest and time,' he said. My boss agreed:
'Elizabeth, take all the time you need.'
That was six weeks ago and I'm still here.
At home, not hospital. And now I fear
the call that must come soon, the voice that says:
'Time's up. You've had your thirty working days'
sick leave. I'm calling now to let you know
you're wanted here at Moonbeam Radio.'

LEARNING HOW TO WAIT

Now that he's gone, I hear the telephone
breaking the silence in a different way.
More silence now than I have ever known.
The noise is louder, more peremptory,
and yet it must be the familiar tone.
The echo, too, might be illusory.
Or do acoustics change when you're alone?

I think at last I'm learning how to wait.
When I was waiting for him in those first
days that dragged on until it was too late
for him to call me, waiting, I rehearsed
our reconciliation: place, time, date.
I knew. Of course I knew that if I nursed
a lost love it would be like nursing hate.

The way to wait is not to, but instead
distract yourself with chocolate and gin.
And keep your diary beside your bed
for afterthoughts and dreams. The discipline
of diary-keeping helped me keep my head
and slow the gushing of adrenaline.
No one will read my entries till I'm dead.

SUBSTANCES

Have they no foolish scandalous selves to quell,
those shunners of cigarettes, gin, poetry?
They need no sweeteners for their brains' nerve cells,
never hazard a day, sleep undisturbed.
Why do they diet for longevity
if all their urges are already curbed?
What can they gain except more time to kill?

A child, I'd try to stay awake some nights
to find out who I'd be if I could keep
a wide-eyed night-watch. Sleepless children deal
in childish things. I craved forbidden tastes
and the unlawful knowledge they'd reveal.
I hungered, thirsted for illicit feasts.
I haven't outgrown my childish appetites.

Addiction is an aid to discipline:
it singles multiplicities to one
vision of preternatural clarity
before the moment of oblivion.
Alcohol and pills and nicotine
gather the tenses of the verb to be
in one time-state: I am-was-shall have been.

FAT CHANCE

Fall? Why do we say fall in love? Love whirled
me skywards in an aerial girlishness
of loving. Hovering, I'd look down and bless
my re-awakening in a perfect world.

Love songs I'd never heard would start to sing
themselves inside my head, so loud and clear
I thought that everyone would overhear
my song of mind and body gladdening.

The song was witchcraft, comedy and prayer,
swan's-wing, delirium and carnal art.
I heard his heart-beat beating in my heart.
The fall comes at the end of an affair.

I felt a part-eclipse of consciousness.
Guilty. Guilty. Loving was my crime.
Songs sang themselves so fast, so shrill each time
I was evicted from love's state of grace.

How could I fall so far and still be sane?
Or not insane? No. Not insane. But now
gin, cigarettes and chocolate allow
pain-free and love-free places in my brain.

I fall in love as gladly as before
but not as heavily. I levitate
as much with gin as love. My extra weight
will break my fall if … when I fall once more.

But I'm less visible now that I'm fat.
No man looks twice at me. A few look once
and I can almost hear them say, 'Fat chance.
I'll never be as desperate as that.'

Women no longer see me as a threat.
They're right. I still fall in and out of love
but most nights of the week I'd rather have
another gin, another cigarette.

SKYLINE

In Memory of George Macadam (1933-2003)

You were the boldest of our group of six
and the most conservative. Five heretics
talked politics and worlds with you all night,
and you apologized for being right.

Defying gravity by your fingertips
you climbed sheer cliffs. You had to come to grips
with absolutes: '*X-S — Extremely Severe.*
But not excess.' Was wordplay a veneer,
a mask you sometimes wore to walk beside
the child you were the day your mother died?

An aneurysm ruptured, and you bled
to death, a long descent. No blood was shed.

You made a world of mountains, clouds and sky,
a world halfway towards infinity.

SEAS' KEEPING

You said you still get sick on the first day
until you find lost rhythms and can sway
with all the moods and mood-swings of the sea.

Beyond all reason are the reasons why
you sail: A kind of creativity?
New worlds of sea and sky when you say goodbye?

Whatever depths and distances you explore
you give your life – This is no metaphor –
into seas' keeping when you leave the shore.

On freighters' radar screens your blip's so slight
it could be flotsam; your navigation lights
vanish between deep wave-walls in the night.

The smaller the craft, the greater the seamanship –
seawomanship – you need; or else you slip
through sleep-lack into fog-brained ocean-sleep.

Salt films the tiller; there's a fine-grained layer
on sheets, rigging and rails. Salt's in the air;
its microcrystals grizzle your black hair.

We're not, could never have been, two of a kind.
You make good speed; I'm doldrummed, far behind,
still waiting for a favourable wind.

MEASURE FOR MEASURE

We can measure the number of snowflakes that fall in a blizzard,
and how many apples there are in a twelve-acre orchard.
We've a program for counting the leaves on the midsummer trees,
and a program for counting the number of fish in the seas.

We can tell to the nearest half-million how many live cells
you still have in your brain. We can say down to N becquerels
just how much radiation's discharged by the sun in a year
and how that affects every atom of earth's atmosphere.

* * * * *

He walks through the blizzard of fish in the orchard: the wizard
who lives at the base of our mind. He was once a winged lizard
and an angel who flew down to earth on a midsummer breeze
of snowflakes and blossoming petals and hymn-humming bees.

He puts sunlight in apples and stardust in humans. His spells
are not witchcraft but pleasure and watchfulness. What he foretells
is the past in the future, the dead in the living, the near
in the far; and the moment of wonder, the moment of fear.

MOZART AND THE SWALLOWS

For Stewart and Judy Conn

A swallow's lungs, a swallow's heart
are too slight to sustain
the long-haul flight from El Aghir
to post-code barns in Gloucestershire:
Slad, Sheepscombe, Miserden.

A swallow has a microchart
that maps the bird's air lane,
ten-thousand-mile-long thoroughfares
from hemisphere to hemisphere
imprinted in its brain.

Mozart heard endings from the start.
And more: he could maintain
a memory of a work entire
while goose quill flew across the quire
notating new terrain.

'Prince? Emperor? I piss, I fart
more sweetly than they reign.
They reign, dear God!' In near-despair
he could do nothing to endear
himself to powerful men.

A swallow's instinct isn't art.
A million-year-old chain
of being leaves it unaware
of how it steers and why it dares
hailstorm and hurricane.

Each voice, each instrumental part –
How could a mind contain
so many strains at once, so clear
and faster than the speed of fear?
Again. Listen again.

NOTES ON ANGELS

Angels have preterhumanly thin wrists
and long thin fingers without fingernails.
Their hands span more than any pianist's.

Angels can have any colour of hair,
but the gold light that glows in angels' heads
is so intense it dazzles dark to fair.

An angel's heartless, for it has no blood.
Its brain is small and yet its mind's immense.
Minding is an angel's livelihood.

Angels cannot choose; they keep vigil
over us incessantly and see
the uses that we make of our free will.

But when an angel pities us, and dreams
of saving us from ourselves, that angel falls
and burns to death. Look. You can see the flames.

There in the clear night sky – A meteor?
Fire, certainly, and from another world:
a fallen angel in a falling star.

When you see a ghost, you needn't fear
the sighting; ghosts don't want to see or hear
their living witnesses. What ghosts want most
is to be seen, heard, recognized as ghosts.

And so, to be an honest exorcist,
you don't need to believe that ghosts exist
or ask if they are deaf or dumb or blind.
But you must trust in the believer's mind.

*   *   *   *   *

Even if your death's unjust, abrupt,
it doesn't mean that you'll become a ghost.
Your flesh will rot but nothing can corrupt
your spirit if it's housed by one good host,
a living mind who keeps your memory:
a lover, say, a child, husband or wife.
Parent and child can span a century
or more. That's a sufficient after-life.

Their natural domains, myth and romance,
are landscapes no map-maker ever draws.
Imagination is their provenance.

What makes the creatures fabulous is the cause
they herald: not the medieval quest
for purity but poetry's skewbald laws.

A poet's mind's a scrabbled palimpsest:
confabulations, fictions, truths and lies
of a fallen angel and a risen beast.

By craft and faith a poet can naturalize
the supernatural and yet conceal
the mystery from unbelievers' eyes.

The absent lover in his mind's as real
a presence as his lover's flesh and blood.
A lover's mind has wounds that will not heal.

And in the province of that sacred wood
he'll see wide-nostrilled, lake-eyed unicorns
when he has learned his own true creaturehood.

THE ART OF VANISHING

Creatures that can't obey the law to kill
and kill or be killed will become extinct
unless they learn the art of vanishing.

Hares practise vanishing by being so still
they merge into the background, indistinct,
unseen because they're part of everything.

Or part of nothing when they wheel and spill
so fast into the past that if you blinked
you'd think the flightless creatures fled on wings.

Wild ponies disappear into a hill
when they graze in deep, blind fissures linked
by rowan, gorse and hawthorn runnelling.

Stags run until their lungs begin to fill
with blood, and run until their spoor is inked
in blood, and run until their gralloching.

But vanishing …? Is it an art, a skill?
Perhaps. It's also timid beasts' instinct,
the starting-point of my imagining.

FLINT-KNAPPER

ROOTS

Thirty degrees: the soil is brick-baked clay.
Flint-knapper's spade blade buckles, fork prongs bend.
Only a crowbar gives him leverage
against sunk rubble paths, lost rockeries.

The crowbar strikes another boulder stone
and jars him from his wrist-bones to his brain.

Flint-knapper fells a hedge of cypress trees.
High hedges leach a soil's fertility
and cast long shadows.
He knows that no birds nest in cypresses.

He chops off branches,
saws the trunks to lengths he can split and burn.

Flint-knapper kneels: he delves and hacks and saws
and levers stumps out by their severed roots.

The last root snaps in a gasp of loosened earth.
He grunts and staggers as he straightens up.

Flint-knapper knows when cypress logs catch fire –
Lilly has bought a fire-guard, finest mesh –
their spicy knots leak resin and explode.

He can hear whole forests thundering.

BEDS

Flint-knapper has learned the knack of tillage and tilth:
spade and fork, and how to chance a day
for his lump-crumbling, sidelong shuffle-dance.
His rake combs, back-combs, topsoil to fine grains.

He seeds the new-made bed,
slakes the soil with rainwater from the butt,
pegs a net against rabbits, wood pigeons
and fat, bed-shitting pampered vermin, cats.

All year round, Flint-knapper has calloused webs
between his forefingers and thumbs.
But a change of tool or task –
the metal-handled log-saw and cypress trees –
can still chafe water-blebs into his palms.

Flint-knapper finds mind's ease can be earned through weals
and the mindlessness of bones' and muscles' aches.

WALLS

Flint-knapper is learning how to make mortar
to fill the powdery gaps in garden walls.
Too much water: the mixture runs away.
Too much cement: the rich, grey, creamy paste
dries to white concrete scars between the stones.
Too much sand: the mortar dries so fast
and loose his thumbnail scrapes it out next day.

'Aw, shite.' Flint-knapper rolls a cigarette.

One afternoon he gets the mixture right,
then wrong, right, wrong, right, right again:
one part cement powder to three parts sand.
He mixes them, and when the parts are one
he makes a crater in the centre,
adds a little water, a little more,
a little more till little is enough.

*   *   *   *   *

Sunday morning: Flint-knapper's up a ladder,
filling gaps between coping-stones.
His task is one part labour, three parts play.

You're driving to the fitness club. Treadmill.
Rowing machine. You time yourself. You swim
ten crawling lengths. You hurry back to the car.

The clouds are high; the air is cool and still.
Flint-knapper fills a gap; his mind's ajar.
This is a perfect day for mortaring.
Inside his head he hears a small boy sing.

BOOKS

Flint-knapper is packing a cardboard box with books.
'I've taken everything I'll need,' she said.
'You'll oxfam the rest of them, won't you, Dad?'

He finds her *Holy Bible*, pocket-size.
He opens it: the print's too small to read,
pages too thin for his thick fingertips.
He doubles it back and hears the glued spine snap.

Flint-knapper carries the last box from her room
to the end of the garden farthest from the house.

He knows it takes great heat to burn whole books
even when he opens them like ridge tents
and props them spine-up on the garden fire.

And so he rips out pages one by one
and crumples them. He rolls a cigarette.
Bible pages are Rizla-paper thin.

The fire is lit. Flint-knapper feeds the flames –
A chair, she called it. A chair in Adelaide –
with twenty ripped-out pages at a time.

It isn't natural, the smell of burning books:
chemicals in the paper and the ink.
Nothing will grow in this corner for three or four years.

HOUSEHOLD GHOSTS

Now that he's alone he thinks aloud,
gives thanks for the habits of the house
and mumbles hushabyes to household ghosts.
Words beyond his will recall themselves:
'Herring, bread and butter, I eat you up.'
One of the ghosts cries out:
'For God's sake, man! Have you lost all sense of smell?'
On other days he hears the same voice sing
a happy apple-picking trug-full song;
and a finger-pointing 'See': a little flock
of teetering goldfinches pecking at thistledown.

She never closed the kitchen diary.
'Hospital 11.30 for X-ray.'
'Holiday begins' and 'Holiday ends.'
Three or four wives together every year.
A week away and he'd lose part of a crop;
beds might dry out or else get choked with weed.

Rain is falling. Flint-knapper's in the shed
cleaning, oiling, sharpening the blades –
'I've seen scarecrows better dressed than you!' –
of loppers, secateurs and shears.
Tomorrow or the first dry breezy day
he'll make another bonfire of her clothes.

SEASONS

The freezer chest in the outhouse has been full
since Esther went to Australia and Lilly died.
He grows more fruit and vegetables than he can eat.

Flint-knapper used to buy his seeds –
leeks, onions, peas, dwarf French and runner beans,
carrots, cabbages, broccoli, Brussels sprouts –
from the main-street seed merchant's until they closed,
and then the ironmonger's shop until it closed.
Now he lets some plants outgrow their season
and he paper-bags their seed.
He chits next year's potatoes from this year's crop.

He prunes in January,
thins hard in May with thumb and forefinger
for fewer, bigger apples, pears and plums.

He saves the weekly *Herald*;
half a page wraps an apple or a pear,
and waddings keep last year's potatoes weatherproof
in their earthed-up clamps.

I hear you sniggering?

His kitchen's scented with a slow ferment
of sugar, gooseberries and alcohol.

When the fuel runs out Flint-knapper will survive.

ACCIDENT

Too big to intercept, the meteorites stun
our planet from its orbit round the sun.

History stops. The stricken planet slips
at first into a glacial eclipse.

And then it fractures. Continents disperse,
small fragments in an infinite universe.

A split world with no gravitational mass
disintegrates in clouds of dust and gas.

A god grown tired of his experiment?
Or just another cosmic accident?

No time to say goodbye, no time to kiss.
You know the world is going to end like this.

THE SECOND COMMANDMENT

'Thou shalt not make unto thee any graven image, or any likeness of anything that is in the heaven above, or that is in the earth beneath, or that is in the water under the earth.' *Exodus* Chapter 20, verse 4

No images? Could Moses have been wrong?
God was a cloud of plagues and jealousy
and hadn't learned how to love in Moses' day.
But why was he afraid of poetry, song,
charms carved from silver, ivory and gold,
a dream of Canaan painted on a board
of cedar wood? And why was God so scared
of being seen if we're made from his mould
in his own image? Afraid we'd re-create
him in ours, and ours would all be false?
Too many of them are, but our impulse
to paint and sculpt is part of the same state
of mind as marvelling. If we reject
that portion of our lives, our gift and need
for image-making, then we make mere creed
of our imagination and intellect.

And when God called for golden cherubim,
rings, crown and golden mercy seat to prove
his godhead, artists worked as much for love
of image-making as for fear of him.

And Moses? He was too busy to suppress
the icon-maker, goldsmith, silversmith.
He had to see in the uncharted myth
imagined ways across God's wilderness.

MAGI

For Richard Price

The magi's journey was old men's wanderlust.
They wanted to restore their trust in stars,
their love of distances.
They thirsted, hungered for the taste
of wine and goat meat in the caravanserais.
They wanted to know if they could still endure
days and nights of desert temperatures
and tell the difference
between a far oasis and a mirage.

When their mission was complete
they went back to their chancelleries and scriptoria
as keepers of the kingdom of written words.
There was no hazarding of dynasty:
genealogies were fixed in cuneiform
along with horses and chariots, camels, slaves,
eunuchs, odalisques and the land's horizons.
The magi never doubted their priestliness.

He was like us until a spirit took
part of his mind. Since then he's had no choice
but otherness: his eyes' demonic look,
some days a streak of frenzy in his voice.

One day he showed us shining squares of clay.
They looked like tablets or flat cakes, not bricks.
Hand-sized. And then in childish chequer-play
he marked one surface with a pointed stick.

The tablet trembled on his hand. 'You see!'
he cried. 'You see? These little marks are words
made visible. Visible memory!'
To me they looked like footprints of small birds.

'These are no hieroglyphs or pictograms,'
he said. He pointed to the wedge-shaped marks:
'I hold a hundred camels on my palm.'
I saw the prints of sparrows, finches, larks.

He pricked another square of clay: 'Ten slave
women, five bolts of silk, and seven jars
of cinnamon. You see. You can engrave
your own accounts of markets and bazaars.'

I looked: more sparrows' footprints, sparrows' beaks.
'No need to trust the word of cameleers,'
he said, 'because these tesserae will speak
the truth. And they will last a thousand years.'

Signs for words that never left my mouth?
My soul's breath trapped in clay? The man was mad.
A thousand years of sparrow-footed truth?
The man was clearly mad, or else a god.

TERRAINS

What drove them to the land of the white bear
where soil thaws for a month and then is lost
again beneath the Arctic permafrost?
What drove them into mountainous thin air?

They fled to lands where no hunter could track
them down. They hid in deserts, rainforests.
They swam to islands made of grey sea-mists
and lived on limpets, mussels, bladderwrack.

Whatever fissurings or fires of brain
or earth forced them from dells of watercress
and lemon groves was a more merciless
geography than their new-found terrains.

Yet even in lands they'd never colonize
but merely cling to, they could hear the sound
of babbling promises beneath the ground:
spirits waking, stirring, about to rise.

They could not know that they themselves had sown
the promises, the spirits in the land.
Deathless? Divine? They could not understand
that all the new-found spirits were their own.

TONGUES

'The speed with which a language can die in the smaller communities of the world is truly remarkable. [...] Within a generation, all traces of a language can disappear. [...] In the 19th century, there were thought to be over 1,000 Indian languages in Brazil; today, there are fewer than 200.' David Crystal: *The Cambridge Encyclopedia Of Language*

We can accuse our neighbours, curse their young,
recall the dead, praise god, crack jokes, tell lies,
breathe 'I love you' in any living tongue.

We say the names of things to recognize
our world, and through a living lexicon
we recreate earth's multiplicities.

Most languages exist as speech alone;
they have no alphabets, no manuscripts.
And when speech dies it leaves no skeleton.

Few languages die quietly. Tongues are ripped
right out. The men and boys are hunted down
for sport. The women live till they've been raped.

Languages bleed to death. Languages drown
beneath white tidal waves. The refugees
must learn the pidgin of the shanty town.

We say the names of things and realize
the lives of living worlds by word of mouth.
A world is lost when any language dies.

HOW TO KISS

Glasgow, Cirencester, Cheltenham –
I go to Oxfam bookshops to buy books,
not blankets, tents or rice for refugees.

Farmers who could be tending fields of maize
are growing roses for Saint Valentine.

Beyond the irrigated fields
the living are too weak to bury the dead.

Blowflies breed in unburied carcasses
and feed on tear-pus oozing from children's eyes.
Catastrophes grow vast in Africa.

I close my curtains on a summer night
to keep out craneflies and small gold-winged moths.

Have you seen swallows kissing in mid-air?
They hover, passing insects from beak to beak.
Swallows have dual nationality.
Mouthed gifts of food were how we learned to kiss.

LULLABY

The dead are simply here, as sure as chance
encounters with acquaintances in dreams.
My visitants don't call me in advance.

No warning, and they come from the extremes
of mind with stories I don't want to hear.
And yet how natural each visit seems.

Absence too is natural: a dead year
might be no longer than a living day.
The dead are different when they re-appear.

And when they change, they tell me to portray
their new identities, their altered states
of being in my neural registry.

Beyond all reason, in my mind's substrate
the dead change me and, changing, I change them.
Together we grow more dispassionate.

But I don't understand the stratagem
the dead are working in me as I try
to shape these lines into a requiem.

All I know is that I can't deny
them living-space. And so perhaps this poem
is less a requiem than a lullaby.

PASSWORDS

Is godliness a separate biotype?
I went to church and counted organ pipes.
You can't find god unless he fingers you;
I sat untouched in my Church of Scotland pew.

If multinationals – the Israelites,
Muslims and Christians – hold world copyright
to true religion, the sacred impulse
I feel when writing poems must be false.

Not false, exactly, but illicit, flawed
if there is no religion without god.
Then I heard Heaney say on Radio Four,
'Poetry is never wholly secular.'

I can't swallow a sacramental host
but my poems play hide-and-seek with a holy ghost.
The impulses that drive me to create
are mysteries, but natural, innate.

A poet's games of hide-and-seek are prayers
for passwords through mind's lowest, wordless layers.
Prayers, passwords, poems and – Blasphemy?
I re-create the holy ghost in me.

'It is only through the psyche that we can establish that God acts upon
us, but we are unable to distinguish whether these actions emanate
from God or from the unconscious.' C. G. Jung: *Answer To Job*

Jung learned from Freud how to personify
by introjection, and then found God inside
his mind but not on earth or in the sky.
God humanized? Or humans deified?

Jung's is the likeliest reasoning I've read.
I can't imagine likenesses of God
because the godhead lives inside my head.
If God were God He'd say Jung's law is flawed.

If He exists only in you and me
and not out there in dogmas, doctrines, faiths,
it's only in our mind that God is free:
all denominations are shibboleths.

We were much too late when we tried to turn
Him to a God-of-love. We'd told Him, 'Kill!'
too many times. We'd told Him, 'Let them burn
in Hell!' He's in our mind. He does our will.

JUST PASSING

I was in the neighbourhood. No, I won't come in.
I thought I'd say hello, pay my respects.

I saw you in the street the other day –
Stow-on-the-Wold, for God's sake. Stow-on-the-Wold.
You had your reasons for being there. I know.

I watched you one hot August afternoon.
You walked, not fast, but too fast for the sun,
trying to follow your what's-it? Follow your stream
of consciousness before the stream ran dry.

And then you thought of me, and felt the heat.
By the time you'd crossed the Square you were wet with sweat.

You slowed your steps. You saw yourself in me
and me in you. You looked your age: old man,
wee boy and all the ages in between.

So there we are. I thought I'd let you know.
I was just passing. No, I won't come in.

LONGHAND

I can feel my illiterate left hand
trying to take over from my right
like a faulty printer with a fuzzy font.

I can't control the areas of my brain
that shape the letters of the alphabet
and so my longhand varies from day to day.

I need to feel a friction between pen
and paper, between pen and fingertips,
between creative chaos and poetry.

And like a child I feel a clearer hand
will make the finished work more readable
than this slow faltering scrawl across the page.

FLICKERING

My brain is flickering like a faulty neon tube.
My diminishing drunk self
is formulating each laborious word
hamfistedly from the big white alphabet
emblazoned on the blackboard in Room 2
of Victoria Primary School, 1944.
On every desk a half-filled inkwell and a dipping pen.

'Silence! No talking. Now you can begin.'

Don't let the small-hours' flickering stop. Not yet.
A six-year-old boy is teaching me how to write.

MESSAGE AND MESSENGER

To be the same person sober, drunk or drugged
takes years of practice and then it takes a night.

In bed I turn my deaf ear to the world.
I never know the moment I fall asleep;
it's instantaneous as a switched-off light.

Through the pillow my fogged half-deaf left ear
hears a doorbell ring and a woman's voice
far inside my head calling my name.

I know I'm dreaming. In my dreams I've grown
closer to realities I can trust:
the dead are living and the living dead.
I need this relativity of dreams.

Neurotransmitters laced with alcohol
change their electro-kinetic chemistry,
change the message and the messenger.

My hallucinations are mainly auditory
and yet the cortex seems to be intact:
a surge of sound when Bach or blackbirds sing.

A simple fear: if I stop tampering
with the natural entropy of my brain,
will I forget I ever knew the song?

A GAP IN THE CLOUDS

Gladness is arbitrary: a gap in the clouds,
a plum tree blossoming, a random squirt
of noradrenaline, a toll-free day.
It can't be earned; there's no entitlement.

And when plum blossom is sparse or snuffed by frost
there are still the apples, blackberries, gooseberries.
Plucking fruits, I feel they are no more mine
than sunlight shining through a gap in the clouds.

SING

If you turn around
and walk with the wind and snow at your back
you can sing in a blizzard.
No one will hear you. I sang. I know.

ON ANY CLOUDLESS NIGHT

On any cloudless night the brightest stars
shine above sparsely populated ground.
Look up, and up. The rhythms of pulsars
are audible, throbbing light. Listen. They sound
like children whispering in a bare-board house
or angels chatting in church ceiling vaults.
The children know their voices might arouse
the beast. Angels might be acoustic faults.

My ear was once as keen as an animal's:
a feral faculty, nocturnal, wild.
Now that I'm half-deaf I hear angels'
voices in the songs of a small child.
The light that radiates from a child's eyes
is self without self-knowledge. Frankincense
and gold and myrrh? Small tokens. The magi's
true gift, too hazardous to analyse,
is the adoration of innocence.

NIGHT-WATCH

In Memory of Norman Thompson

Sailing among islands in the night –
The Orkneys, the Little Minch and the Inner isles –
I take the flashing pulse of far-flung white
from unseen lighthouses, and through the kyles
the stone's-throw beacons' winking red-eyed light.
Shipwrecking rocks are near but out of sight.
We're cruising lightly over black sea-miles.

In fact, the lights are logged in computer files,
with charts and stars. We steer by satellite.
And yet just being here again beguiles:
this night-time voyage is a little rite
of passage. Passage? Pilgrimage? Exile's
a state of mind. My night-watch reconciles
the elements of darkness and delight.

ISLAND

LANDFALL

He threw his sword and shield into a lough
and boarded the currach as a barefoot commoner.

Sea charts were prayers and the helmsman's lore.

His island landfall was the place of his resurrection.

In his second life
he sought out tribal shrines and spoke to their gods.

LARKSONG

We wanted to taste the breath of the saint
when we entered the Abbey thirty years ago.
We found those effigies:
the two who seized clan lands when *clan* meant *family*,
and paid a mason in stolen silver
to sculpt eternal life into their carcasses.

When we walked in sunlight across the clovered grass
to view the cemetery of kings and queens –
Irish, Danish and Norse as well as Scots
all jostling for a share of his sainthood –
there was larksong in the air.
The cemetery was chunks of weathered stone.

SANDERLINGS

With heavy rain and an east wind on our backs
we by-passed the Abbey and walked to the west shore.
No one else was there.
Eleven shingle-dancing sanderlings
were singling invisible shrimps out of the stones.
We watched till we were drenched and shivering.

FORECASTS

I can't imagine the geography.
Met Office men and women speak too fast
on BBC Radio 4 for me to see
the whereabouts of the weather they forecast.

Anticyclone, frontal system, trough:
I can't keep pace. I can't make mental maps.
I know my hearing isn't quick enough.
And Radio 4 forecasters leave no gaps

Between their rushing words and sentences.
Speaking at a speed of a hundred miles
or more per second they fog all distances:
London, The Wash, Carlisle, the Western Isles.

You know the way you stop for a closer view
of a bookshop window or a building site
and then forget to look, forget you're you
when memories spontaneously ignite?

The Isle of Harris, Iona, the Long Mynd,
Oslo, Innsbruck – I walk in thunderstorms
with you. Soaked by the slanting rain and wind
we walk a little faster to keep warm.

The bongs … And radio news at six o'clock –
Famine, football, murder, war – is more
predictable then the weather on a walk
round Loch an Eilean in April. Let it pour!

POTASH PLACES

'A force-9 gale.' Force-9? In the Little Minch?
The captain said he couldn't take the risk.
And so all day the ship sailed up and down
the Sound – Tobermory, Tobermory – the Sound of Mull.

Thick mist is climbing the cliffs at Mullion Cove
and overflowing the cliffs' edge and the path.
I can't see where the precipice begins.

The river's sources in the Ochil Hills
are slight until the rivulets link up
to make the gouging river that made the gorge.
There was a laddered, handrailed river walk:
a rockfall made the gorge impassable.

In Painswick churchyard, counting the close-trimmed yews
I lose count again at the bed of stones,
small squares set close and spirit-level flat.
Chiselled names and dates are sharply etched.
The stones must cover urned kilos of potash
or bodies buried upright to save space.

Too much loose potash will poison any soil:
scatter my ashes sparsely on Inchmaholm.
Or anywhere. My place of last resort
is in your mind: there's nowhere else to go.

Wood smoke is visible for miles on windless days. The scent of wood smoke doesn't drift far; not for humans on a still December morning. But I smelt smoke, tasted it before I saw the bonfire at the edge of the coppice.

Mature hazels were orchard-like in their pruned and random orderliness. A good crop, not cob-nuts but bundles of long straight poles stripped of their side-branches, lay beside the path. Saplings of ash and birch and sycamore had been sawn off at ground level; self-seeded since the last pollarding, they would have made a wilderness of the coppice.

A man was burning a mound of prunings: easing, raising, aerating the upper layers of ash, birch and sycamore with a long-pronged hay-fork. He was playing at burning, playing seriously with the fire, coaxing, teasing, prodding flames from the smoke.

I walked slower, enjoying his play. Twenty yards was a fair hailing distance between the track and the fire, between me and him. And slower still … Fifteen yards, ten yards … Too close. I should have called out, 'Fine day. Fine day for it.'

I stopped and said nothing. He shuddered. He turned and saw me watching him. I was too sudden a stranger. His big face twitched, twitched, twitched, twitched before it found fear, a childlike anger and fear.

'Fine day,' I said. I smiled. 'Fine day for it.'

I had breached the world of a dreaming child. The bonfire was his alone. I had trespassed and I owed him recompense.

'I love the smell of wood smoke on a winter morning,' I said. My face smiled again. 'Bonfires. The scent of prunings burning. The smoke and the flames.'

His expression changed. His big face beamed, admitting me to his world.

'Andy says I'm to burn all the brash.' He pointed into the coppice. 'Hear the chain-saw?' He turned to the bonfire again and prodded it. 'Was a bugger to start this mornin. The fire. Too green. A bugger. So Andy gives it a skoosh out the petrol can. Skoosh!' He cackled with laughter. His laughing face was too young for his head. 'A skoosh.' He gestured. 'And whoosh! Up it goes!' His laughter seemed too high-pitched for his big round head. 'Andy says we're here another two-three days.'

'Two or three days? I hope the weather holds.' I heard my voice call out, 'Good luck with the burning.' I raised a hand and smiled and walked on.

I can still hear his wild delighted laughter. My words weren't recompense for my intrusion. That morning was his. The bonfire was his alone. I hope the flames he conjured from the smoke have burned me from his memory.

BRAIN SCANS 1998

For Maurice Lindsay

HYSTERIA

You hated, and your hatred scraped forty years
of poetry from your tongue. Rage stripped your face
of its thin layer of humanity.

You panicked. Your brain was so full of fear
there was nowhere left for mind; there was no space
for consciousness to keep its tenancy.

You felt so sad you couldn't resist despair's
corrupt, voluptuous embrace
of thought and language, self and sanity.

Infantile, that chaos in your hemispheres.
Infantile but without the grace,
without the innocence of infancy.

Live now on the safe side of frontiers
and practice anonymity.

MIND-READER 1

The patients signed the forms, agreeing to take
enough only to block out pain and dull
the sound the saw made cutting through the skull.
The patients volunteered to stay awake
and talk to him as he probed their open brains.
He needed more than damaged tissue, malign
or mutant cells; he was trying to assign
functions to places, trying to map terrains
in living patients who were well and sane
enough to play this cerebral hide-and-seek,
conscious enough to speak to him. *(So speak,*
for God's sake. Speak! Before the cortocaine
wears off.) He moved the tiny stainless steel
electrodes once again. 'What do you feel?'

MIND-READER 2

Tumours, lesions, encephalopathies,
the merest aneurysm in a vein
that leads blood through the networks of the brain –
sound-waves trace differences in density
between malignant tissue and benign.
A kiss of matter and anti-matter scans
the brain for Alzheimer's or Parkinson's
disease, for signs of faults in the design.
In my case it was just an inner ear,
a labyrinthine anticlimax. But if
there's a next time I'll go back – half-deaf,
lopsided with tinnitus, grey with fear –
to the machine and trust it with my flawed
brain more readily than I'd trust a god.

IDENTITY

An accident? Not quite, but I hadn't planned
on being like this. Identity redesigns
itself, its selves – my selves – along lines
I didn't choose and still don't understand
even now. There's fewer of them now,
fewer than the good, bright selves I've lost,
but there isn't one among this lot I'd trust
with another's life. Not one of them knows how
to be at peace, or simply to ignore
the others, let each other be. Instead,
each wants the others exiled, silenced, dead.
Who do these little bastards think they are?
I know. But how can they …? Or how can we …?
How can this be all that's left of me?

SUB-PLOT

I sit in silence listening to the chords
and rhythms of Bach and Bartok, Bird and birds.
I do most of my thinking without words.

What seem like dialogues inside my head
are sense impressions; nothing can be read
into them since nothing has been said.

Raking, spiking a lawn – that loosened state
of mind and body is lost when I translate
mowing, spiking into the alphabet.

My brain decodes a million stimuli
unthinkingly. The pupils of my eyes
dilate, contract involuntarily.

And there's the sub-text, or rather, the sub-plot:
I do most of my thinking without thought.

CANKER

The flaw offended me.
I rubbed at the canker in the apple wood,
trying to finish the piece before the light failed.
But each new pass of the rasp
and each new cambium level exposed more decay.

I put away the tools
and then I waited, staring at the thing in the half-light.

Layers of sweat cooled to a single layer
as cold and heavy as a leaden shirt.
The sweat grew cooler still;
I felt a cold, dead skin beneath my skin.

For hours the after-image flickered on and off:
brown fungus spreading through the pale wood.
A phantom self inside me assumed a crouching stance,
hunched over the bench,
muscles tense in his shoulders, wrists and hands.

Because I'd stood too long at the task,
too long, and too rigidly intent on finishing the piece;
because I'd worked against time
and the times and weathers in the changing widths of the grain –
because of these things my body bent itself
and neurons fired their futile little flares
all evening round the canker in my mind.

MISTLE THRUSH

A mistle thrush was my way through the darkness
of Castle Hill wood. The notes were streaks of light
in the January dawn. Through eight winters
the bird's song was a charm against madness.

The six short phrases of the mistle thrush
are more than the thousands of pages I wrote
in that sick institute,
processing words, reprocessing processed words
until language was meaningless.

The poem is wrong because the bird and song
were formed so long before we lost our wings
and fell from the tree. Or fell, God's afterthought,
from the sky, or the tree in the sky.

When I try to find words for the song
the bird stops singing.

I haven't heard the cycle of six phrases
sung as a single song. The mistle thrush sings
three of the phrases, and then five, and then two,
changing the order so that the sequence sounds new
each time I listen.

I listen, but I can't memorise the song.
The song has no beginning and no end,
and so the poem is wrong.

I hear the thrush singing through sleet and snow
and flailing branches of a winter gale.
In spring's dawn chorus it's the soloist.
I hear it sing alone so late into the night
that I can barely see the silhouette,
the bird a black corn dolly
on the black haystack of the holly tree.

I wake and fall asleep to the song of the thrush.

THE VANISHING PARAKEET

Say a word aloud. Say *parakeet*
aloud. Say *parakeet* aloud again:
parakeet. And once more: *parakeet*.
The parakeet begins to moult; the bird
begins to disappear into the sound.

Mouth *parakeet* as if aloud, with lips,
tongue, throat, teeth – *pa*, *ra*, *kee*, *eet* – *parakeet*.
The twittering screech is barely audible.
Your mouth is silencing the parakeet.
The sound is disappearing in the word.

Parakeet. Another *parakeet*
till *parakeet* is no more than a set
of tiny muscles flexing, facial nerves
twitching, twitching. And a synapse pulsing
automatically in your brain.

Parakeet. The word's now meaningless,
silent – *parakeet* – invisible:
a perfect hiding place for parakeet.

THOMAS HARDY
AT STINSFORD CHURCHYARD, 1927
For Andrew Johnstone, Douglas Kilpatrick and George Macadam

CENTURIES

The churchyard is so full of death
that what was once a level ground,
an acre reclaimed from the heath,
is now a place where two great mounds
are growing from the earth beneath.

They rise like two green hills, each crowned
with stones that look like monoliths
or tumuli. The hills confound:
it is as if the sunken paths
do not lead to the church but round

And down into the green hills' myths
of skulls and crucifixes, down
and down to the bare bones of faith
where centuries of death are bound
together in the living earth.

WHAT THE GRAVEDIGGER SAID

'Ashes to ashes ...' Padre opens his fist:
the ball of loam bursts with the little gasp
and scatters across the oak lid like the rasp
of scurrying rats. Padre says 'Dust to dust.'

The sound of it, the sight of where we all
must come, can twist a mourner's face from grief
to terror. An afterlife? Aye, after life
the body lies beneath a ton of soil.

You ask again – 'The body after death?' –
as if you already knew and wanted now
to match my lore against yours and see how
far I'll trust a stranger with my truth.

The knowledge seems unnatural, unclean
to those who are so fearful of the facts
that follow death, yet they are gentle acts
of cleansing. Let me tell you what I've seen.

As soon as the heart stops beating it begins
to rot from the inside. Maggots and worms?
They can't do beeswaxed oak or pine much harm;
coffins decay like corpses, from within.

I've seen the little deaths, and I see why
the knowledge of them sets a man apart
from other men. Some call it a black art
to know the ways of bodies when they die.

Black or white, an art or craft or trade –
call it what they will, they all come here
for that last gentle cleansing. Year by year
I care less for the living than the dead.

WHAT THE GARDENER SAID

A day of darkness and light
and all the shadows between morning and night.
A day of skies
and then the fashioning of boundaries
of oceans, lands and lakes.
And in the same day, before man, woman or snake,
there was the making of trees.

Until our forfeiture
of the dream, trees were the earth's first creatures,
the wisest and loveliest.
We adorned the great oaks and the yews, dressed
them with skulls
and slaked their thirst with the blood of the white bull.
We were children of the forest.

We forfeited the dream
for our awakening to iron, fire and time.
A sleepless sky god
taught us new laws of life and death, of good
and evil, promised us love
if we would take fire and iron into the groves.
We felled and burned the woods.

What we could not kill
we called superstition, then folly, then child's play until
May pole and May Queen,
Mummers and Morris Men, Green Man and Jack-in-the-green
danced between the new faith
and the stumps and smouldering ashes of the heath,
between scrubland and fen.

The trees, sir, in this arch
that stands between the graveyard and the church;
these yews are seeded from
parent plants older by far than Christendom.
And all our christenings
will not wash away the knowledge of these things.

Sir, the skies are darkening.
You say that you have reached the end of your search?
I wish you safely home.

WHAT THE STONEMASON SAID

Frost and wind and time and rain
on granite, sandstone, slate or marble
write their dead languages and garble
God's words and mine.

Rain and frost and wind and time
on marble, granite, sandstone or slate
wipe away the age, the date
and the dead name.

Time and rain and frost and wind
on slate, marble, granite or sandstone
gnaw until their work is done
and my words end.

Wind and time and rain and frost
on sandstone, slate, marble or granite
pronounce the only lasting rite
in words of moss.

Geese are flying from one feeding ground
to another, an easy inland flight
and yet the birds are calling ceaselessly
to keep their pace and height, to keep their tight
formation like a skiff of visible sound
trailing its audible wake across the sky.

Nearer, I can hear the separate cries,
alternating notes of different pitch
that rise and fall in fluctuating streams
of rapid overlapping rhythm. As each
goose calls in time so the geese improvise
their variations on original themes.

Goose music is a roll-call against squalls
of hail, a counterpoint against the long
darkness. Goose music is itself a force
of nature and the geese are syllables
in a fugue that's two-in-one, both song
and winter flight across the Stirling carse.

NIGHT SNOW

Big, wet flakes were falling fast and straight
out of the void into the ring of light.

I looked so long at the fast-falling snow,
letting my field of vision come and go –
from the white surface of the window ledge
to the black shape and shadow of the hedge,
and upwards from the disappearing grass
to the surrounding dome of nothingness –
I looked so long at it I couldn't tell
the snow that was illusory from the real.

Snowflakes fall like snowflakes in a dream
of time; like particles of time they stream
in a continuum of here and now.
Yet even as I watched, the fallen snow
was melting into the past. Snowflakes fall
like visible silences that overspill
from gardens into streets until the white
soundlessness of snowfall fills the night.

Big, wet flakes of snow were falling thick
and fast and randomly, but by some trick
of repetition and multiplicity
the randomness grew rhythmic, orderly.
And by some trick of movement through the night
sky, thick flakes fell slower till their flight
became this hovering, half-lit from below,
this ceaseless, stationary, fast-falling slow
delirium of silence, time and snow.

AWAKENING THE TREES
From the Journal Of Patrick Napier

THE COMPANY OF TREES

No, I do not believe that trees have souls
But I enjoy the company of trees.
I am as much a creature of the forest
As of the town. No, I do not abhor
The heathenism of the Indians
Or the Métis.

                I write this in my book
But dare not play denials with the man
Lest I disturb my hibernating beast
And find it more ungovernable than the God
Whom Monsieur Taillandier cannot forgive.

PLAGUE CARRIER

I came ashore like a refugee from plague
And found the fever was already here,
Urgent, unslakeable and driving me
From place to place until there was no doubt:
The malady was in my mind; it fouled
My thoughts like poisoned water in a well.

Tic and tremor in my eye and hand.
Anger and sadness. Anger and sadness. Waves
Of sundering anger. And my thumping heart
Absurdly alternating Charge! Retreat!
Troughs of extravagant, unfounded grief.
My dry throat palpitating like a frog's.

IN THE COMPASS OF A TREE

I leaned against a maple tree. I closed
My eyes and breathed as if I were asleep
In the cool scented compass of the tree.
I heard the pale leaves moving in the wind
And whispering distantly like audible stars.
I felt the intricate simplicity
Of purpose in the tree. I opened my eyes
Again but I was still asleep. I saw
Beauty in the irregularities
Of trunks and branches, buds and leaves and crowns
Of maple trees, and walnut, elm and oak.
I saw the trees' benign indifference
And knew it was companionship enough.

And since trees have neither minds nor souls
Their beauty cannot be a state of grace.
They are a form of unregenerate life
Lower than creaturehood and yet above
All other things. How strange that trees should be
Not supernatural but natural.

FROST

Trees are seldom wholly silent or still.
In the great frost, the coldest I have known
Since my first voyage on *Challenger*,
When nothing moved and the whole land was dumb
With snow, I heard faint creakings in the trunks
Of sugar maples as the frozen sap
Expanded. I remembered the small sounds
Challenger made at anchor in the night.

'Listen. Do you hear him?' the Indian said.
'The spirit of the tree cries out with cold.'

THAW

The spirits weep with joy, the Indian might say
Of ash trees on a day like this
When April sunlight is just warm enough
To thaw the hoarfrost on the leafless twigs.

I am content to feel the melting frost
Drip on my head and on my upturned face
And in my eyes as if the tears were mine.

THE FORGETTING OF SONGS: WHAT THE INDIAN SAID

To forget the forgetting of songs.
River. The song of the river. Forget.
The song of every tribe of animal and bird and tree.
The song of the stars. Forget. The stars. Forget. The moon.

We sang the songs. Sang. Sang the songs.
Songs sang in our mouths
And we knew the path that would lead us through the forest.
Singing. And across the icefield. Singing.

Lost. Forget the songs. Whisky. Lost.
Whisky to forget the forgetting of the songs.
Whisky. Swallow forgetting. Swallowing.
And fall again into the whirlpool.

The whirlpool is Jouskeha singing.
Singing the swallowing song that drags me down
And down with all the animals and birds and trees.
Down. And falling stars. Down. And moon. Falling.

Song? Song of songs?
Sun-song before the whirlpool?
Whisky and sun-song before the forgetting?
And then the whirlpool. Swallowing.

Jouskeha's swallowing song, the whirlpool.
Sun-song? Forget. Forget.
Jouskeha's song of unmaking. Forget. Forget.
Swallowing all for the forgetting of the songs.

CURING THE INDIANS

The willow man, the keeper of the songs,
The healer, the astronomer and the priest –
The Indian told me how his kinsmen died:
One taken by wolves, and one crushed by a tree;
'Eaten by tree' is what the Indian said.
Another entered the river and was drowned,
And one was seized by a thunderbolt, he said.

The Indian is deranged by alcohol.
He jabbers in wild English, Iroquois
And a third tongue no one has heard before.
His every utterance is fantasy
Or lamentation, like those Highlanders
Whom we left weeping on the quay at Leith,
Too drunk and broken to board the *Belvedere*.

And then the Indian spoke as if one man
Had died these deaths, died and returned to life.

'C'était une résurrection toute païenne,
une participation mystique,'
Taillandier said. 'Maintenant ils sont guéris.'
He smothered his grunt of laughter in a cough.

'The river,' the Indian cried. 'The river is red.
On other days he says the river runs black.
Cured, by God? The Indians are cured?
He says he can no longer find his way
Alone through the forest. 'The trees,' he cries,
'the trees are changing places in the night
and when I waken everything is lost.'

DRAWING A TREE

I dip my pen and try to draw a tree:
A round white cloud is anchored to the earth.
I try again: ten fingers, crooked, black,
Of someone buried alive. And once again:
A lacework of black veins and arteries
Reaches from heaven to earth. I dip and draw
A weeping birch: the Indian's long black hair
Makes him an animal without a face.

AN OAK MILLENNIUM

Now that I have some French I am unsure
Of Père Taillandier. What I had thought
Was righteousness now sounds like epigram.
He told me the oak he felled last week
Had stood five centuries. Could this be so?

'Napier, vous êtes un homme sans châines.
Deux chênes, et voila votre millénaire,
Le paradis terrestre dans les arbres.'
A smile. He ridicules me, or himself?
A grunt of laughter smothered in a cough.

I asked him why his men had felled the tree.

'Le paradis, c'est un grand encombrement
a l'église.' Like curing Indians,
I thought. Again the smile, the little cough.
Not cynicism but complicity?
With Indians and Métis and with me.
And with the forest? 'Pas un encombrement,'
I mumbled in reply, 'mais l'église même?'

Five hundred years felled in a single day.

'Peut-être, Napier,' Taillandier said.
He neither smiled not coughed as he turned away
And walked back to his little wooden church.

AWAKENING THE TREES

The Indian asked if I would go with him.
The wind was fierce. There was a racing moon
And yet the air surprised me with its warmth.

In each black oak a set of organ pipes –
Echo and solo, swell and great and choir –
Played bass to treble simultaneously.

And through the branches of the hazel trees
The fluctuating melody and drone
Of bagpipes playing pibrochs in the night.

'Jouskeha is awakening the trees,'
the Indian sang, and he began to dance
a shuffling little dance in the April night.

I shuffled, too. I heard his moaning song
Among the moaning oaks. 'The trees,' I cried.
'Jouskeha is awakening the trees.'

Patrick Napier was commissioned in the Royal Navy from 1873, and
served as a sub-lieutenant on HMS *Challenger* on its voyage to the
Antarctic in 1874. When illness forced him to retire from the navy in
1881 or 1882, Napier spent some years travelling in Canada before
returning to Scotland in 1889.

EDWARD THOMAS:
EMBARKATION LEAVE, DECEMBER 1916
For William Paxton and John Thomson

CATHEDRAL

The smell of many candles snuffed,
darkness and then the sickly waft
of molten wax with that charred tang
of desolation on my tongue.
I think of bodies burned to ash,
of bodies gutted and the flesh
embalmed. I think with every breath
I take I taste the spores of death.

I knew I would find nothing here
but did not guess at such despair
as this. In the cathedral gloom
the smooth grey sandstone pillars gleam
like great beech trees in the half-light
between heaven and earth, bearing the weight
of fear and faith. I make my way
beneath the beech wood's canopy.

THE PATH THROUGH THE WOOD

Mosses are spreading and small grasses growing,
hollows are filling up with fallen leaves
and only the worn stony places are showing
the narrow course the path makes through the trees.

Whoever trod this path has gone away.

I walk alone, without maps, lingering
for birdsong, running water, otter's spoor.
Yet I seek more than these; I am hungering
for demons of the glade, the gorge, the tor.

I would be pilgrim but I cannot pray.

Demons? I seek no ordinary haunting
by ghosts or gods but creatures natural
and earthly as I am. I am hunting
an order of creation before the fall.

With neither maps nor faith I go astray.

The wood is growing dark. I walk on, casting
no shadow on my wayside shrines of white
birch beside the half-seen path, trusting
the thrush that's singing in the fading light.

Then have I chanced on a lost trysting-way?

Even as I make my last thanksgiving
at the wood's edge, I know I shall not find
stillness enough; more and more I am living
in the sundered country of my mind.

I have walked the goodness out of another day.

RAIN

An hour ago when I resumed my walk
this upstart river on its bed of chalk
and loose flints was a dusty Shropshire lane.

Skies darker than the earth have come so near
that steeples, towers, treetops disappear.
I lose my landmarks in this new terrain.

Thunder is quarrying the cliffs of heaven;
there is no nesting place for dove or raven.
I think the world will never be dry again.

The only source of light is the flickering tongues
of the celestial snakes, the only songs
their gasp of hunger and their roar of pain.

My feet are churning soil to mud and slime.
I walk in darkness on the edge of time.
The end should come in heavy and lasting rain.

IN THE MIDDLE OF THE WOOD

This stillness in the middle of the wood
is just as true and natural a force
as the west wind that flows around the elms
at the wood's edge. No bird has hardihood
enough to fly or forage in that fierce
power, and yet it cannot overwhelm
the still centre. Instead, the wind's subdued
by stillness, baffled by it, turned off course
to circumnavigate the little realm
that is unruffled in the buffeting flood
of rushing air and is itself a source
of the simplicity I need, the calm
at the storm's centre, stillness neither good
nor evil in the middle of the wood.

WALKING HOME

It wasn't the storm clouds mustering
in a night sky with neither moon nor stars,
    nor the December wind blustering
across the sodden fields and through the sparse
    hedgerows. It was a festering
sore of my own making, an exile
in the long estrangement of that final mile.

I walked on in my covering
of sleet and rain. The comfortable sweat
    had chilled and I was shivering
with cold and the cold fear of how complete
    had been the last mile's severing
of task from purpose, the journey from the goal.
I felt the frost spread outwards from my soul.

I was a child again, mumbling
'The Angel Gabriel' through my chittering teeth
    but the sleety wind was fumbling
at my numb mouth while brain and gasping breath
    and feet were stumbling
the frozen measures of my self-deceit,
each to a different, stiffening slow beat.

The Loughton fields were glittering
with ice when I reached home. The kitchen fire
    was still alight and sputtering
with little tongues of singing flame, a choir
    of glowing coals unfettering
the spirits of a forest that had drowned
a million years ago. Dear ghosts, I found
    such warmth in your chattering
and hope of homecoming however far
I have to travel in a world at war.

THRESHOLDS

To come in from the garden's summer light
and think you've crossed the threshold between sight
and nothingness because each room is blind
with smoke ... To wake up in the night to find
your pillow soaked in blood, your mouth, your nose
sticky with blood and yet to wonder whose
the blood can be ... To listen to the pitch
of your voice rising, breaking in a screech
of puny rage ... is to know these intense
wild bits and pieces of experience –
so vivid that they seem hallucinatory –
filed instantly as long-term memory.
And know year after year your mind will stage
black comedies of smoke and blood and rage.

THE CODE

They're no more ours than the flock of waxwings
that broke their flight just long enough to tear
the last few berries from the whitebeam trees
across the street. And when the trees were bare
the birds flew off into skies darkening
with winter dusk at three in the afternoon.

They're no more reasoning, our memories,
and no more ours than waxwings migrating
not randomly or wilfully but drawn
by the turning angles of the sun
and by the indecipherable code
implicit in the cells of brain and blood.
Memories come and go, not when we ask
but like the waxwings in the winter dusk.

MOURNERS

Grief is a lesion. Networks in the mind
are ruptured, and the broken ends of thought
and fluttering hours come crowding round the wound.
The women carry flowers, bulbs and pot
plants, water, thick new candles in glass bells,
tins of polish for the metalwork –
the lattices of black wrought-iron scrolls
around the graves – and little weeding forks
and hand trowels. The wound will never heal
completely but the kneeling women make
a quick unthinking task of death until
the agony of grief dulls to the ache
of time beginning again, and mind and life,
and grief becoming the memory of grief.

THE VICTORY

In Memory of Alexander Scott, M.C. 1920 – 1989

'Done is a battle on the dragon black.'
You spoke as if the poets could win back
our nationhood, and the land's life or death
could be decided by the poet's breath:
Soutar, MacDiarmid, Henryson, Dunbar.

I pressed you once about your earlier war.
You waded through the dying and the dead
to reach the shore. Wounded, you would have bled
to death beside the men of your platoon
rather than give up the ground you'd won.

And when the enemy had you by the throat
at last, you joked in whispers and you fought
so long that by the end you'd found a way
of death that was another victory.

THE FONT
In Memory of Ronald West, 1934 – 1994

You apologized for having grown so gaunt
that you were the living ghost of Ronald West.
You wanted us to see you were possessed
by peace as well as death. You didn't want
to see your ghost reflected in our eyes.
You were as gentle an apologist
for death as you had been a celebrant
of life and craftsmanship. You knew the font
that pressed words to the page and yet released
them into space. And you could civilize
the most barbarous texts with your imprint.
Dear visitant, I'm glad you've chosen to haunt
me for a time and help me recognize
the gift of goodness when a good man dies.

THE INHERITANCE

The war, the hospitals – he was away
so long he was a stranger when he died.
I knew his face better from holiday
snapshots than from the life; and when I tried
to weep there were few tears. Later, I thought
I owed him part of my life for the years
he lost and for his early death. I ought
to have known that my father re-appears
in me no matter what I think: I feel
about books, craftsmanship, woodlands at dusk
just as he once did, his coded will
decoded as I sit here at my desk
translating impulses that might fulfil
my father's purpose and complete his task.

A poem doesn't exorcise its ghosts.
Instead, they pass at will across the coast
of conscious and nonconsciousness to haunt
me with the same old fears and guilts. Ghosts won't
be bound, go by the book or treat a script
as something they must stick to. I accept,
willingly now, that even when I think
I've found words for a poem's missing links
they hover on the edge, only half-heard,
like the far cries of migratory birds.

I'm hunting for the creatures in the hope
that I may never fall into the trap
of catching them. The long hunt would be lost
if a poem wholly gave up its ghost.

SECOND NATURE 1990
For Cara, Nick and Norma

IN THE NORTH

Light fades slowly in the long evenings of May and June
here in the north. My eyes adjust
and when I straighten up from a seedbed
I can still make out the darker shapes of swifts
against an archipelago of clouds
and the outline of a thrush
singing from the top branch of a plum tree.

I feel the stiffness and the aching satisfaction of tasks.
I put the tools away
while I can still see the path to the outhouse.
Indoors, I switch on the light
and wash off the stains of earth and calomel dust.
The thrush calls out and I look from the window
onto an incomprehensible darkness.

I stare until I see the deeper mass
of apple trees and plum trees
and the boundary wall,
black shapes with nothing between them
except the glint of glass in the greenhouse
and my reflection out there
waiting like another self at ease in the night.

STARLINGS IN GEORGE SQUARE

A black leaf on a leafless tree
begins to sing, and thousands more
join the harsh, high-pitched, off-key
November vespers in George Square.

They leap into the air and swirl
in a blizzard of false notes among
the leafless trees. George Square skirls
with shrill November evensong.

They wheel and screech, a multi-track
fast-forward scratch falsetto choir
of thousands, a November flock
of starlings singing in George Square.

SWIFT

The note stretches across the sky.
I look up but faster than my seeing
the bird has flown far from the sound
that soars and dives and doubles back on itself.

Dazzled with summer light, I look for it
where it can't be, then swift and cry collide
in that long *Hree*, that whetting of sickle blades
heard with the scalp, the scraped spine.

Swift twists, thrills, swoops out of itself,
a black unpredictable mobility
hurtling from scream to scream,
scoring dark after-images against the light.

Swift dives in tapering clamorous shapeliness
through panic into shrill perfection.
Swift flies through high-pitched perpetual summer
and never comes down to earth alive.

Someone in the Department of the Environment
sees farther than I can, claims the white patch
will bring a boat from the island.
I turned the signal board and hooked the latch.

Waiting is easier in a place like that.
I stood on the crazy paving of the pier
and looked at the island in the lake.
The hatred I'd brought with me began to clear.

Even on my first visit I'd felt
in that landscape of green and blue-and-green
the illusion of familiarity:
I recognized a place I'd never seen.

The beating of the engine – I heard the boat
before I saw it – grew firmer, like a normal pulse.
The same man stood in the stern, handling the craft
as if he, or I, or it were somewhere else.

The ruined priory prompted the ruined words:
religion, heritage and history.
We need the dull excuse because the truth
of lakes lies much too close to fantasy.

It's as if lakes and islands were outlined
in us before we see them. They fill a space
already mapped out for them in our mind.
An island in a lake's a dangerous place.
Without looking for them you may find
some other ruined words, like peace, or grace.

LAVENDER, FIRE, QUEENS

The lamp above the lintel
was too small for so much darkness.
The door was unlocked, just as she'd said,
and when we opened it and called her name
we heard the echo in the passageway.
Hand in hand we followed the sound of our voices
up the stone staircase, across the gallery and into the light.

She had left the curtains open.
You sat beside her in the window seat
and I saw stars shine through your far reflections.
I heard your voices
saying herbs and pottery and hives
like two off-duty druid priestesses.
You spoke as if I weren't there.

When you laughed and leaned together
strands of her hair caught in yours and yours in hers.
I heard your voices saying lavender, fire, queens.
And when the strands drifted apart
I saw your reflections out there, your backs towards me.
I said nothing, afraid you'd come in from the night
with your lips, your tongues dripping with honey and flames.

DIGGING

The grip and thrust of spade,
the measured lift of loam
on which the turning blade
prints its curve and gleam,
the pause, the thrust and then
the rhythm returns again.

The circulating blood,
the beating of the heart
and the steady flood
of breathing become part
of the one rise and fall,
one rhythm and interval.

And there are some days when
I dig and dig until
the weariness creeps in,
until I cannot tell
if the rhythm I divine
is the earth's pulse or mine.

PICKING SPROUTS ON A WINTER MORNING

I walked into the grey half-light
and put the wood pigeons to flight.
They had been tearing at the crowns
of the plants, and I sometimes found
on the leaves where they had perched
their frost-blue shit like oil paint fresh
from the tube.

        I would stand stooped
over the plants, running my chapped
hands round the stalks until I had
a picking. I churned the soil to mud
between the rows on mornings when
the frost thawed, or when sleet or rain
fell while I picked that week's crop.

And when at last I straightened up
I felt the cold and the small hurts
not as a price to pay but part
of a blessing that's familiar
and yet so rare, come from so far
across my mind and from a past
so distant the gift would be lost
were it not for the rain and sleet,
hands raw with frost, wood pigeon's shit
and the wood pigeons in flight
through winter morning's grey half-light.

FROGS

A frog, climbing a sunlit wall,
climbing slowly towards a crevice,
stopped, upright, motionless so long
it seemed emblem of frog, the paint still wet.

From a bonfire of prunings a frog jumped,
a slow curve through still air, and then was lost.
Minutes later the same slow arc of frog leaping
away from flame into the greenness of grass.
Later, another leap, slower, heavier.
And then a long stillness around the cackle of fire.

Clearing weeds from the edge of the long path,
the hoe slicing through layers of gravel
to loosen the lush growth,
I saw it just as the blade struck.
Stiff, dry, hard,
it was stretched longer, thinner than any I'd seen.
A botched mummification of frog.

Yesterday beside a plum tree
one jumped out of my footprint
and then waited, surrounded by strangeness,
like a crouching pulse.
When it jumped again
into the long grass and out of sight
it left its image there,
the lacquered iconography of frog.

A VERSION OF BEOWULF

On the second day you asked for *Bee Hunter*.
Your eyes were still bruised shut behind swollen lids
but the pain had cooled to an ache of tender flesh.
I saw you were beginning to enjoy
the sense of safety growing round the hurt,
enjoy, perhaps, those few days' sightlessness.
I sat on the edge of your bed and began to read.

The ship must become a creature of sea and stars
to make true voyage and landfall;
the trail of blood and slime leads back to the swamp;
treasure and dragon gleam in the same cave.
And each must be entered, cave and swamp and ship –
the inescapable law enacts itself –
so that there may be order in the land.

I stopped reading. There was so much blood
I thought the book might be too much for you
after the accident. You were lying back
on the high pillows with your eyes shut tight;
you were so still I thought you'd fallen asleep
with the sound of my voice. And then
you wriggled upright and asked me to read on.

How can they survive that weight of law?
How can they accept it and still survive?
Unless they know denial will unloose
the disenchantment more wasting than plague or war
and only the enormity of their belief
gives order in the land; perhaps their way
of wrapping a sense of safety around the hurt.

The jewelry and the armour and the swords
seem charged with inexplicable properties
when they are truly given, truly worn or won;
not symbolism or magic but a lost
order of reality and law.
Grendel and dragon? Did we kill off these things
or do we call them different names?

My son asks if I'll read to him again
in the afternoon. Again I feel
the book's too much for him, too real, too near.
Perhaps he simply wants to hear my voice
lapping the silence, reading him anything.
I look at his swollen lids and I agree;
I need his few days' aching sightlessness.

(*Bee Hunter* by Robert Nye)

I WATCHED YOU WALKING

You were walking across the lawn.
I had been reading in the summerhouse
all afternoon, and when I looked up
you were walking across the lawn towards me.

I watched you walking: with each easy stride
you were stepping in and out of the past
like a ghost through walls,
casually in and out of then and now.

The loose green jacket you were wearing,
the pleated skirt, sunlight again on your hair –
I remembered the first time I'd watched you walking.
You smiled and waved as you came closer.

You stepped in and out of twenty years,
walking away from them and yet bringing them with you,
the you of then so easily in step
with the you of now. You waved again.

It took me a few seconds to respond
before I grinned, waved back, and dropped the book,
startled at being recognized by both of you
and through so many walls.

From HELOISE AND BABINGTON

TRAVELLER'S CHEQUE

'I should have sat in the shade or called a taxi.
My hand was shaking as I signed the cheque;
my signature a childish forgery.
The teller looked at it and asked my name.
His voice was far away.
The word stuck in my throat;
a buzzer pulsed and tingled in my head.
He asked my name again.
I listened to the slurred echo of my voice
trying to say Babington. Babington.
He asked again.
His face grew faceless.
I watched the grille shrink to a dot of light
like the instant before a television screen goes blank.
And then that long whining bleep.

'Just a sunstruck Englishman cashing a traveller's cheque.
But there was a touch of finality that time –
a shuffling of feet, muffled urgency of voices,
a bumping like a little boat at a jetty.

'I opened my eyes and you were there;
Beltran, too, somewhere, but mainly you.
And so much sky above your head.
I thought this is it, Babington. This is it.
And so it was, but not the one I thought.
I think I babbled a bit; I'm not sure.
You brought me back to life, Heloise.'

'Not back to life so much as down to earth.
But yes, you babbled, Babington,
quite beautifully about your second life
and the safe crossing you had made.
I said, "I placed your money in your pocket book
between your passport and your driving licence."
I felt a slight regret when the babbling stopped;
you have not been so lyrical since then.'

'No? If it's hot enough this afternoon
I'll try to cash another traveller's cheque.'

AVALANCHE

I was eleven and in love with Casoni.
I stood at the finishing line and watched her
come from a cloud of ice like a priestess.
Casoni was sixteen. I was possessed, Babington.

For a year I lived inside my love of Casoni
like a sparrow in a glass cathedral.
I spoke of it to no one.
I began to hate my parents – the way they dressed,
the way they talked, the way they ate their food.
And then I grew afraid of my hatred.

Love and guilt and fear and hatred, Babington.
All this from watching Casoni ski.

I watched, and there were two of her:
Casoni of the high slopes
swooping down through her avalanche of laughter
with that fierce and lovely mobility,
and the other Casoni, a sacred corpse embalmed in my love.

Later, I felt unclean in my empty cathedral.
Puberty, of course, Babington.
And hunger; I felt so hungry I entered the world again.

I did not wish for it, that possession,
that desolate ecstasy of adoration,
and would not wish for it again.
But it had its moments of divinity,
like a great illness.

COUNTING IN THE NIGHT

Sometimes like a saxophone in the underpass.
Or two saxophones, a dialogue of saxophones
inventing a music that plays between sleep and waking.

And sometimes it was counting in the night
when my skin was slippery with pain
and squealed against the sheets when I tried to turn.

Some nights I grew smaller than the pain;
not pain in me but me inside the pain
like a cat in a sack.

I hissed out broken bits of childsong.
I stuttered on unpronounceable prayers.
And then I would count.

One hundred, Babington.
When I reached one hundred. Then.
Or fifty if the pain was too much.
Fifty at least or the sack would close on me.
Not fortyeightfortyninefifty
but forty-eight, forty-nine, fifty.
Lose count and I must begin again.

Fifty made a little gap in the pain.
I could reach a hand through it, an arm
and press the button.
Then. Music would play its indulgences.

PARACHUTE MUSIC

It is not simply the wind whistling in your ears;
there is the helmet and the visor and the jump suit.
I wear my ski suit, the red one, and ski boots.
That way parachute music sounds hollow,
far away, Babington, but not faint.

You have seen newsreel of De Gaulle?
You remember the sound he would make,
like humming or clearing his throat
before he began to sing *La Marseillaise*?

Last week they gave me a red smoke canister.
In my red suit, trailing red smoke,
I was a comet, a falling star.

But it is better without it, the smoke;
better when I leave no mark in the sky
and think of nothing else all the way down
but myself in space.
Then parachute music ends in a gasp of arrival
and the creation of the world.

CHOOSING A DEATH

'If you were to die today, Babington,
how would you choose?'

'I have a choice?
Then I'd die in your arms, Heloise.
Or better still, at your feet.
Yes, at your feet. And you?'

'It would be winter, late in the afternoon.
I would go walking in the snow
until I could walk no more.
I would lie down and close my eyes and listen to the stars.
Soon I would be insensible.
They would not find me until the spring.'

'It wouldn't work, Heloise.
The whole village would come looking for you.
And you wouldn't freeze; the snow would melt around you.'

'I would undress.'

'Then that's how I'll die –
naked in the snow at your feet.'

'You choose well, Babington.'

ENGLISH TALK

'Then is there nothing your regret, Babington?'

'I heard some English voices the other day.
I'd joined Beltran for a glass of wine
on the terrace of the Kohnizberg.
Two English couples sat at the next table
and one man said his garden would be a jungle
of goose-grass and cuckoo-spit when he got home.
I could feel the goose-grass tugging at the hairs of my arm
and the little gobs of froth on the backs of my hands.'

'Homesickness, Babington? Regrets?'

'Fears rather than regrets, Heloise.
I'll be found out soon and asked to leave.
I'll wake some morning and find
your car and all your clothes gone.
Or come back tired or drunk some night
and find that everything has disappeared –
the house, the field, the barn, the walnut trees.
And in the village Moulle will frown and say
"What house? There never was a house up there.
There never was the woman you describe.
Such a woman? She is the woman of your dreams."
I'm sorry. This is silly. I've said too much.'

'Silly? Too much? That sounds like English talk.
Come, Babington. We shall search the field and orchard
for your goose-grass and cuckoo-spit.
And if the house is still here when we return
we shall go whispering from room to room
like new inhabitants,
listening to the echoes of our voices
and the little creaks and sighs of the house.'

'I think I was wrong about Moulle.
He would say, "That woman? She is a Witch."'

SETTLEMENT

'Sometimes I hear noises in the night,
little creaks and groans and murmurings.'

'Yes, Babington. It is settlement.
I used to hear it when I came here first.
I used to search the house for intruders,
or mice or a shutter in the wind.
Nothing ... until I went back to bed
and then the murmuring began again.

'I asked Moulle if there had been tunnelling.
"No tunnelling," he said. "Nothing like that.
We had an earthquake once, but very small;
we didn't know until the evening news."

'And just when I had decided it was ghosts
a builder came to repair a window frame.
"There has been settlement," he said;
"I fixed the same one thirty years ago."

'Settlement, Babington. Isn't that comforting?
The house speaks to itself. It speaks to you.
Tonight when it begins you must speak back.'

'There, there, old house. I hear you. Settle down.'

'With you I can imagine growing old.'

GARDENERS

They look up, smile and wave
to us in the passing train.
Such childlike make-believe
from adults is insane.

Not gardeners, of course,
but trusted simpletons
allowed to work outdoors
on flower beds and lawns.

And trustingly they grin
beside the railway track;
they smile and smile within
the meaning of the act.

I turn back to my book
and try to find my place;
instead, I see the look
of glee on one man's face.

Defective and yet real,
not make-believe, the sense
of joy the gardeners feel
behind their boundary fence.

REMBRANDT ON LIGHT

For Stewart Conn

Gentlemen, you must be stricken by light.
For some of you it will be like falling in love.
Love, gentlemen, imperious love, the kind
of love that brings vertiginous days and nights
when you ransack your broken memory
for the image at the centre of your mind –
her lips, her eyes, her hand, or even her glove –
and find nothing. Or find crude forgery,
moustachioed Gioconda with a squint
in both her eyes. You think you will never paint
again. And then, when lacing up your shoe,
you see the loved one smiling down on you.

Men have been transfixed by heavenly light
as Saul was when he felt the wrath of God
strike like a thunderbolt that left him blind
and helpless for three days until his sight
was given back to him. Then he could see
into the life of things, into the mind
of God. A three-days' blindness on the road
to anywhere is a small price to pay
for perfect vision ransomed from a dark
night of the soul. But Saul turned saintly clerk,
a holy scribbler, gentlemen, who chose
to squander the vision in a mess of prose.

Gentlemen, you must admit the light
more readily than the love of mistresses
or faith in saints. Practise the craft, let in
the particle of fire that will ignite
both heart and brain in the one loving faith
in light, then you yourself are the origin
of light and maker of its mysteries.
You are the agents of the secret truth
and craft of light who can redeem this brief
uncertain life into that second life
through which a loved world shines in death's despite.
Gentlemen, be cautious of that light.

ASKING THE WAY

I wouldn't have asked him,
wouldn't even have pulled up
but his tractor was at a standstill,
the engine idling, rooks circling,
and he was rolling a cigarette.

He stood by the fence
and began to tell me how to get there
before I'd said the name of the town.
I asked him how he knew;
he spat a shred of tobacco from his tongue.

'You'll get there before them,' he said.
'Before the crowd comes out. Football.
The football match.' He didn't look at me;
a slow movement of his head took in
the half-ploughed field and the November sky.

Wellington boots and dungarees,
the jacket of what once had been
a best suit, and a flat cloth cap. He turned
and for the first time met my eye
and read the look I hadn't known was there.

Tractor and car, the engines idling,
the rooks cawing and circling …
He spat the cigarette butt from his mouth
and stared till I wound the window up
and drove on, wishing I hadn't stopped.

ANTARCTICA
From The Journal Of Patrick Napier
For Robert Nye

The weather continues calm but the terrain
Is more mountainous than our charts show
And we have travelled but seventy miles
From where *Challenger* lies at anchor with half-crew.

Mountains, charts and compasses conspire
To make a phantasm of the natural world.
Some charts are false and all are incomplete;
Our compasses' erroneous reckonings
Suggest the Pole has fickle satellites
Whose only constant is inconstancy.

By tricks of distances and wind and light
The mountains seem to march across the land,
Shouldering their way through flying clouds.
Mountains enormous on the morning skies
Dissolve in minutes in a sea of mist.
The mountains come and go at will, as if
This land has not assumed a final shape.

*   *   *   *   *

We have seen distant turmoils in the air –
Too far, too swift for our camera –
Like great flocks of birds startled in their flight.
And on the ground, towards the horizon,
We have seen upsurgings and scatterings of snows
As if creatures fled from us in panic.
And yet there are no other creatures on this land;
Only our small company of men and dogs.

At night when the dogs have ceased their howling
I hear the rending of the ice
And the land groaning under its burden of ice.

From the ratings' tent I hear the sounds of a melodeon.

Sir John allows the lamps to be kept lit all night
In the three principal tents and in the latrine.

*　*　*　*　*

On the sixth day the skies were overcast.

The Esquimaux dogs were ill-tempered
And were whipped snarling to their traces.
The gale got up while we were travelling.
It lifted grains of ice from the ground
And hurled them in our eyes.
I could not walk against the force of the wind.
I felt the gale pressing my eyes into their sockets.
I could not see the sledge ahead of me
And tried to call out to Captain Russell
But the words were blown back in my throat.

The dogs lay down in the snow and would not go on.

*　*　*　*　*

The gales have kept us tour tents five days and nights.
I fear the tents will not take the onslaught.

Last night Sir John said, 'Gentlemen,
I cannot believe this land is part of the Creation.
This world of ice is not of the Lord's making.
Perhaps another god …'
I could scarcely hear him speak above the gale,
Its long blasts like the harshest organ chords.

'Perhaps this everlasting wilderness
is how the world was before there was God.'

*   *   *   *   *

The gales have lessened and we travel again.

Each day is a wailing twilight of winds and snow,
Each night a broken sleep of racing dreams.
I dreamed that great white apes
With swollen members glowing in the darkness
Ran round and round my tent.
I dreamed I stood engulfed in a wild storm
On the shore and cried out as I watched
Challenger in fair weather set sail for England.

And all this time the clouds are come so close
We have seen neither sun nor moon nor stars
For seven days and nights.

I no longer hear the sounds of the melodeon.

The snow and ice lie so deep that we walk
Not on the earth but on solid weather.

We walk on the weather of many centuries.
If engines could be brought to this land
We might sink mines down to the beginning of time.

*   *   *   *   *

Yesterday a man, a sledge and a team of dogs
Fell through the snow into an abyss.

Atkinson was lowered on the longest rope.
He saw nothing; heard no cries from man or dogs.
We tied together all our ropes
And lowered him down again for a full hour,
Calling out to him all the while.
When he came up again he said there was nothing.

Sir John said, 'The abyss is bottomless.
The creatures have fallen into infinity.'
Captain Russell said, 'No. But we have lost
William Carter, a most honest and willing man,
And with him one third part of all our food.'

That same night Russell said we must turn back.
Sir John said, 'My dear Russell,
I knew you lacked all sense of mystery
But I had thought you a bolder man than this.'

'Sir, we lack not mystery but food.
If we turn back tomorrow we may live.'

                *   *   *   *   *

The men grow careless on the journey back
And inattentive from lack of sleep.
They are less companionable to one another.

Some men do not wax their boots. One man
Has forgotten how to make fast both tent and sledge.
Another, Rawlins, acts as if the dead
Carter were still one of our company;
Greets him, stands aside to let him pass.

Captain Russell is intolerant;
He speaks harshly, insultingly, to the men.

'You think me hard, lieutenant,' the Captain said.
'Do you not see that each day we take longer
To make and break our camp?
Each day we travel less and less
And yet we eat the same quantities of food.
We may yet perish in this land.

'The men grow careless with their lives, Lieutenant.
I see in unwaxed boots an end to walking
But there are many miles between us and *Challenger*.
I see in an unfastened tent an unfastened mind,
Admitting the cold, admitting death.
Rawlins is not in mourning for his dead friend
But in love with death itself.
Rawlins is accompanied by death;
He has found that sweet delirium which, unchecked,
Will prove contagious.
Soon the men will wish to lie down in the snow.'

*　*　*　*　*

I dreamed I could not sleep for fear of the beast.

When I awoke and saw the little lamp
And the shadows waltzing on the walls of the tent
I felt the joy of being alive:
I walk in this vast mercilessness and survive.
I am in communion with every man
Whoever travelled in this land.
We are a brotherhood of Antarctica.

*　*　*　*　*

I found Rawlins lying dead in the snow
With a smile frozen deep into his features.
We wrapped him in his sealskin coat
And heaped snow upon his body.

Captain Russell stepped forward and raised his hand.
Surely he cannot scold them now, I thought.
Another scolding will send these men to their deaths.

'We have lost another good man, a cruel loss,
for we are less than two days' march from *Challenger*.
Less than two days, and then I promise you
Hot mutton pies, hot dumplings, pints of rum.'

*　*　*　*　*

I saw *Challenger* in the bay but felt no joy.
I heard the men speak of their deliverance
And hurrah the Captain and Sir John.
I watched the men dance a hornpipe on the shore.
They beckoned to me but I would not join them.

* * * * *

I have my journal but it does not catch
The pitiless majesty of that land,
The changing vastnesses and the many musics.
Will memory smooth away the mountains and abysses,
Diminishing the continent to a chart?
I pray that part of me is still falling
Through the bottomless abyss towards infinity.
And I pray that I have loved and feared
Antarctica enough to have its dreams.

* * * * *

Sub-Lieutenant Patrick Napier served on HMS *Challenger* which sailed
to the Antarctic in 1874 under the command of Sir John Murray.
William Russell was Captain of the Marines on board.

NEWS AND WEATHER MAP

Over and over, through the squall
of sleet they flew from the thorn hedge
into field's icy acreage –
snow buntings with their twittering call.

The television news that night
showed pictures of the latest war,
scenes from another massacre,
the little houses still alight.

Bodies of women, children, old
men and the gathering cloud of flies –
the commonplace atrocities.
Meanwhile, the younger men patrolled

With a battalion in the east
where they were hunting to the death
a people of a different faith.
The antics of the killing beast

Still horrify, but when I viewed
them I felt no more sense of shock
than when I watched the twittering flock
of buntings foraging for food

Or testing weather for the flight
back north. The television map
showed sleet and snow and the cold snap
continuing with no end in sight.

FIGURES IN A MEADOW

Three figures in a meadow: man,
hardy little mountain horse
and child, a girl of nine or ten.

Harebell, clover, meadowsweet –
the meadow is more flowers than grass,
a meadow chirring in the heat.

Voices drift; the man and child
are speaking only to the horse
that glistens in the shimmering field.

The heat is visible: mirages
are scribbling on the liquid air
above rosettes of saxifrage.

Fumbling with tenderness or fear
she grooms the horse with her open hand;
the man is fastening the gear.

Beyond the meadow, currents waft
up through the lisping aspen leaves
like semaphores or heliographs.

The man is tightening the girths.
Dragonflies are hovering
like iridescent hieroglyphs.

He mounts and turns towards the far
cold mountain places without paths.
She watches till they disappear.

SPHERES 1975

For Norma

She walks the corridor, and holds
her papers tight against her breasts;
she sits near the door, and folds
her sheaf of notes until they rest
upright on the desk, her screen
against a world she does not trust.

She is afraid of being seen,
afraid of where a look might lead
or that a whispered word might mean
much more than she had really said,
afraid someone might burst the cage
of fear that she has come to need.

I watch, and then begin to wage
the gentlest of campaigns. I speak
as if I knew and could assuage
the terror, and I softly take
away the bars, page after page.
Her mouth moves and begins to make
a shape that could be joy or rage.

MULL MOUNTAIN

Wild strawberries grow from the crumbling cliff face.
I pluck one tiny fruit
and particles of rock gone soft with age
disintegrate and turn to earth again.
Perhaps this mountain would unmake itself
if there were time and strawberries enough.

STIRLINGSHIRE GARDEN

All airports closed, he said,
and snowploughs lost in drifts
and the world running late.

Here rooks are ferrying sticks
from lawns and shrubbery
into the soaring beech.

ISLAY LOCH

There was nothing that would attract water
on that flat expanse of moor, nowhere
for rain to run, for streams to flow or gather,
and yet the improbable loch was really there.

It shone with an opaquely amber glint
a little way across the level moor;
I set out on a faint sheep track that went
through feather grass and heather to the shore.

There was no track. There were no other sheep.
And all the earth's irregularities
opened and closed around my stumbling feet;

around my head hung a cloud of horseflies.

From time to time the loch was out of sight
before I reached the edge eventually;
I saw the shifting sediment of peat
make water look like whisky or pale tea.

Appearance and reality appear
to be like interchangeable extremes
when smooth turns rough and the opaque grows clear.
Across an actual moor where far is near
an amber and unlikely loch still gleams.

BEANS

Leaves are thinly spaced on the thick square stem.

And flowers come
like wings of butterfly from chrysalis,
pale fans of silk unfolding from black hearts.

Summer is the scent of flowering beans.

Pods swell and grow fat and stiff with fruit.

The split pod is an ocean opening.

The green stones
are fashioned by the swaying flow
of slowly lapping tidal centuries.

The beans are lapidary smooth.

On innumerable
minute white fibres tipped with dew,
on a layer as fine as misted glass, they lie.

Autumn flowerings are brief, and without scent.

LANDSCAPE WITH LAPWINGS

Another April and another day
with all the seasons in it, with lapwings
falling out of sunlight into rain,
stalling on a squall and then tumbling
over the collapsing wall of air
to float in zones of weightlessness again.

And on a day like this in such a place –
a few square miles of moorland in a round
of rounded hills, rain clouds and scattered trees,
with water flowing clearly over stone –
in such a place I feel the weights slip off
the way a lapwing would if it were me.

The place might form a frame of reference
for calculating weightlessness, and all
the weathers that are in one April day,
for drawing what conclusions can be drawn
from lapwings tumbling in and out of light
with such a total lack of gravity.

MOWING

Concerned again to get the first line straight
and all the following lines,
I take a long look at the holly tree
beyond the farthest corner of the lawn.
The image fixed, then I am drawn
along the imagined track across the grass.

Yes, I suppose it is the old concern
for order, and the need
to make a pattern that might contain
at least some of the fear, the need to print
a small perfection that I cannot take
elsewhere beyond the boundaries of grass.

If I can cut the first swath straight, the task
seems to complete itself:
a steady spray of green with the odd trace
of clover, daisy, speedwell and pearlwort
flows from the blades; I simply hold the mower
on alternating lines of angled light.

And at the end I see that here and there
a line has gone astray.
The little imperfections lead me back
into the sense of time that we call real.
Next week I'll try again, but now I breathe
the perfume of burnt petrol and cut grass.

PRUNING

I clench my fist and see the bright blade slice
through the brown stem of the raspberry cane
in a dry cut, diagonal, precise.

My daughter follows me along the rows
and gathers up the severed stalks, the plain
raspberry prunings, because she knows

That even the harvesting of withered things
can satisfy, and that there still remains
the fiercer pleasure of the great burning.

She stares into the blazing berry-bright fire;
summer goes up in flame and smoke again
as we feed it, cane by cane, to the autumn pyre.

SAWING

He clutches firmly at each branch to catch
each separate section, and to feel the flow
of tremors tingling through his tightened fists.

I force the pace so that my son can watch
the sawdust spilling like a fall of snow
and see the flurry gather into drifts.

As we stack the logs and brush away the patch
of dust, I feel the aches begin to grow;
my son still sees the flakes of falling snow
and feels the saw-strokes throbbing in his wrists.

PLUM TREE IN MAY

The newest twigs are dark and twisted, seem
much older than the lower, thicker bows,
yet from these wrinkled little sticks somehow
the flowers emerge, a sprinkling of pale cream
about the tree. My image of the spring
is this cold, scentless, lovely blossoming.

ELM TREE IN SEPTEMBER

The rounded autumn moon was masked behind
the moving branches of the crooked elm.
My blurring vision, or perhaps a trick
of interplanetary light? The realm
of stars or elms trees or my giddy mind?
O pale mandala in a dark cleft stick.

ASH TREE IN DECEMBER

Leafless, of course, and now against the snow
the ash tree seems more black, more surely dead
than when we passed this way an hour ago.

I try to break a branch, and a thin spray
of powdered snow showers down upon our heads;
the black branch moves but doesn't come away.

I tug again but the ash tree will not yield.
We turn away, our shoulders garlanded
with snow, and my hands branded with bright weals.

SOUNDS BEFORE SLEEP 1971
For Norma

BONFIRE

A flame bursts from the fire
like a scarlet bird in flight,
hovers then disappears
in the November night.

The crimson conjurer
and all his fluttering tongues
charm the children near;
they laugh then leap back, stung

By licking flame and smoke;
firesbreath is in their cries,
and bird and crimson cloak
are burning in their eyes.

A sixpenny rocket trails
its hissing yellow arc
across the night, then fails
down through November dark.

Briefly the dry leaves flare,
the little rockets flash
faintly. The children stare
but flames have turned to ash.

The conjurer is still
and the scarlet bird is lost.
We shiver in the chill
of the November frost.

They think of sleep, they turn
towards the house and there
tonight their dreams will burn
with images of fire.

CHILD AND CHRISTMAS TREE

A dry December; sun and moonlight shine
together about your head, Caroline,
making your beauty more than beautiful.

I rise, cross to the window, and pull
the curtains close. The tree and fairy lights
draw you, smiling, to the bauble-bright
corner of the darkened room.

We need our jingling charms against the gloom,
the applause of paper unwrapped from a gift.

You cry and point; I rise again and lift
you up to the tree, to something far
beyond your grasp. The bell? The tinfoil star?

You smile and lean towards the star and touch.
Tinfoil stars are just within our reach.

MORNING WITH MIST

I cannot see where the trees begin
in this loose thicket that fills the morning,
this spillage of darkness into a day
where nothing has substance.

Slowly it silvers, begins to glint
with floating particles of freezing light,
and a black stalk drifts from the iridescence
to become a tree, and a tree and a tree
until there is a far blur of woodland.

The stuff dissolves, slips, seeps away
with only a hint of frost on the wet grass
and, amongst the trees, a smear of smoke
or the breathing of some great gentle beast.

SUNDAY BUS

He heaved himself into the bus and filled the aisle.
He wore a brown tweed cap, a stiff black suit.
There was a dull greased sheen on each black boot.

He sat beside me and I saw his hands,
the stained hands of an iron-moulder, such
hard hands they could have no sense of touch.

But in the corolla of his cupped hands
he held a small bunch of anemones, hid
or cherished them, violet, pink, red

Petals gleaming round the dark dark hearts.
The bus stopped. He heaved himself from his seat
and got off at the cemetery gate.

THE LAST CLEAN BOUGH

Each day that summer he walked the avenue
of elm and hawthorn to the broken orchard.

He put his saw to the dry boughs and he thought
of autumns full of fruit, of blossomings.

And he remembered a girl, a night when leaves
moved in the wind and moonlight silvered her.

But that was fifty years ago … Now
the house beyond the orchard was a shell.

The orchard wall had fallen stone by stone
and the fruitless trees had fallen: apple, plum,

Damson, cherry, pear – the pear tree where
the summer moon had found the silver girl.

The girl beneath the tree beneath the moon
was long since dead. What had they said

That summer night beneath the pear tree where
now he puts his saw to the last clean bough?

He shoulders the branch and walks the avenue
of big elms and sparse hawthorn hedge.

In his garden he drops it on the pile
of timbers stacked against the coming frost.

HOUSE WITH POPLAR TREES

At the far end of the towering poplar lines
his house soars. From the upper window
he oversaw his land, his farms, his mines.
He watched his poplars and his slag-heaps grow.

The earth, the coal beneath the earth, the air
above, whatever breathed the air – yes, these
hirelings bonded at the yearly fair –
were his. Behind his screen of poplar trees

The place still stands today. The entrance hall
is deep in daisies, buttercups, rough grass;
the main doorway has fallen from its wall
in the crumbling remnant of the roofless house.

Nearby a dim-eyed unworked Clydesdale feeds
on what was once the lawn. You'd think a breeze
might bring the ruin down, or moss, or weeds,
behind the screen of towering poplar trees.

Did it show, he wondered, when a word
they had deleted slid into his mind?
No, not possible; no, it was absurd.
But the word stuck to his tongue. Might he not find
the sudden heartbeat could be overheard?

The little man who asked him for a light
that morning called him friend and made a joke
about the president. He had to bite
back the smile from his shut lips. Men who spoke
like that might come back quietly in the night.

White waters reaching up a warm shore –
he'd heard or overheard someone saying
it was like that. But he knew that the whore
beneath him on the bed was listening
for footsteps, voices, fists on the outer door.

At night he dreamed of burning till the heat
woke him. He sat up and struck a match
and thought of the little man who joked. Sweat
cooled and he crossed to the window to watch
policemen in pairs patrol the empty street.

Down there in a few hours more, among
the thousands who would look once and then walk
on, the man who joked might come along
with other men, invite him for a talk
and see the marks of burning on his tongue.

Worple Press is an independent publishing house that specialises in poetry, art and alternative titles.

Worple Press can be contacted at:
PO Box 328, Tonbridge, Kent TN9 1WR Tel 01732 368 958
email: theworpleco@aol.com.
website: www.worplepress.co.uk

Trade orders: Central Books, 99 Wallis Road, London E9 5LN
Tel 0845 5489911

TITLES INCLUDE

Against Gravity – **Beverley Brie Brahic**
(A5 Price £8.00 ISBN 1-905208-03-0, pp. 72)

'graceful, sensual, smart'   *Thomas Lux*

Full Stretch – **Anthony Wilson**
(Price £10 / 15 Euros ISBN 1-905208-04-9, pp. 104)

'work shaped by both wit and compassion'   *Mark Robinson*

Bearings – **Joseph Woods**
(A5 Price £8.00 / 10 Euros ISBN 1-905208-00-6, pp. 64)

'his work shows an impressive reach and range'   *Eiléan Ní Chuilleanáin*

A Ruskin Alphabet – **Kevin Jackson**
(A6 Price £4.50 ISBN 0-9530947-2-3, pp. 88)

'you may like to consult *A Ruskin Alphabet* by Kevin Jackson, a collection of facts and opinions on ruskin and Ruskinites, together with a variety of pithy remarks from the man himself'   *TLS*

Paths of the Beggarwoman: The Selected Poems of Marina Tsvetaeva – **Belinda Cooke**
(A5 Price £12 / 18 Euros ISBN 978-1-905208-11-1, pp. 144)

'a wonderful book'   *Liam Carson*

'a profound sense of authenticity'   *Joy Hendry*

Looking In All Directions – **Peter Kane Dufault**
(A5 Price £10.00 ISBN 0-9530947-5-8, pp. 188)

'Wonderful stuff' *Ted Hughes*

The Great Friend and Other Translated Poems – **Peter Robinson**
(A5 Price £8.00 ISBN 0-9530947-7-4, pp. 75)

Poetry Book Society Recommended Translation

The Verbals – **Kevin Jackson in Conversation with Iain Sinclair**
(A5 Price £12.00 / 20 Euros ISBN 0-9530947-9-0, pp. 148)

'Highly interesting.' *The Guardian*

'Cultists will be eager to get their hands on it.' *TLS*

Stigmata – **Clive Wilmer**
(A5 Price £10.00 / 15 Euros ISBN 1-905208-01-4, pp. 28)

'a brilliant piece of work which brings honour to our time'
Sebastian Barker

Buried at Sea – **Iain Sinclair**
(A5 Price £12.00 ISBN 1-905208-06-5, pp. 104)

'the power of a genuine wizard' *Michael Moorcock*

A Suite for Summer – **John Freeman**
(A5 Price £10.00 / 15 Euros ISBN 978-1-905208-10-4, pp. 78)

'His poetry re-awakens a sense of wonder in us' *Kim Taplin*

To Be in The Same World – **Peter Kane Dufault**
(A5 Price £10.00 / 15 Euros $20 ISBN 978-1-905208-07-4, pp. 94)

'as fresh and valuable as ever' *George Szirtes (Poetry Review)*